JUNKANOO
Festival of The Bahamas

E. Clement Bethel
Edited and expanded by Nicolette Bethel

Paintings by Brent Malone

MACMILLAN
CARIBBEAN

First published 1991

Published by MACMILLAN EDUCATION LTD
London and Basingstoke
Associated companies and representatives in Accra, Auckland, Delhi, Dublin, Gaborone, Hamburg, Harare, Hong Kong, Kuala Lumpur, Lagos, Manzini, Melbourne, Mexico City, Nairobi, New York, Singapore, Tokyo

ISBN 0 – 333 – 55469 – 8

Printed in Hong Kong

A CIP catalogue record for this book is available from the British Library.

Cover illustration is from a painting by Brent Malone which is the property of June Knight, Nassau.

Contents

Preface

The caringly scholarly work by the late Clement Bethel on the Bahamian festival of Junkanoo has provided us with an invaluable guide to one of the most definitive expressions of the Caribbean region's collective creative imagination. Through this book, his daughter, Nicole, has no less caringly preserved for posterity a Caribbean social and cultural testament revealing the dynamics of formation of a still emerging civilisation forged out of of the cross-fertilisation of transplanted cultures over the past 500 years.

The Bahamian festival stands authoritatively beside the Trinidadian Carnival, the Mardi Gras of New Orleans, the Carnaval of Cuba and Rara of Haiti, the Masquerade and John Canoe of the Leeward Islands and Jamaica respectively, as well as the more recent Hosay festival that followed on the arrival of Indian indentured labour into the West Indies when slavery finally came to an end in the late 1830s.

They have all inspired a number of academic studies and published accounts, many of which seek to place the annual events in their correct perspective as manifestations of the genre of festival arts which are the result of collaborative action by the mass of the population as cultural response to and interaction with new and less hospitable social environments. The Caribbean region has known not only suffering under enslavement and colonialism, after severance from ancestral hearths and involuntary exile, but also survival by way of the triumph of the human spirit over all odds.

All this is still relevant today. Bethel's work on Junkanoo was itself in response to issues of identity, of the groping for cultural certitude and the imperatives of nation-building following the achievement of political independence in his native Bahamas. The invocation of 'democracy' by founding fathers went beyond the polling of votes in emotion-charged and periodical elections. It also took into consideraton the energy and power encased in the collective creative imagination and the age-long efforts by the people from below to see to their self-affirmation through periodical outbursts of artistic activity manifested in the composition of music, the confrontation of harsh social realities with the wit and humour of oral poetry, or the un-restrained expression of freedom through dance.

The appropriation of such gifts by native post-colonial political directorates in search of ways to consolidate the legitimation they acquired through the polls, provided for the ancestral popular festivals new space and a sense of purpose in the new dispensation. Heritage tourism and the celebration of national achievement have been served by Junkanoo which, as Bethel reminds us, has been used to celebrate anything 'Bahamian', from the homecoming of Sidney Poitier, the celebrated Bahamas-born movie star, to an election victory. The Prime Minister of The Bahamas 'jumps' Junkanoo on Boxing Day each year to the delight of his constituents.

Perhaps this is as it should be for any concept of power without taking into account the organic underpinnings of the rich collective intellect and creative imagination of 'the governed' is the surest guarantee for failure of Caribbean development in the foreseeable future. Both Nicole and Clement Bethel would see their own publication further confirming that.

Bahamian Junkanoo continues, then, as part of that repertoire of creole (native-born, native-bred) expressions giving to humankind opportunities for access to new modes of aesthetic energy and artistic experience.

This book is timely and all the more welcome for this very reason.

Professor Rex Nettleford
University of the West Indies
Mona, Jamaica
April, 1991

Acknowledgements

The production of a work such as this would have been impossible without the help and encouragement of many people, and it would be similarly impossible to list them all. There are some, however, who deserve special mention for their contribution.

First, Brent Malone, for his patience, his generosity, and his art, and for his continuing commitment to this project. My father's choice of him as collaborator on his book was no accident, and I have found working with him an undiluted pleasure.

Next, Dr Gail Saunders, for allowing me the use of her various studies, especially her PhD dissertation, and for her overwhelming support. She plied me with useful information, provided advice when I was stuck, and was my goad when work slowed to a stop. Also Dr Keith Wisdom, for the use of his PhD dissertation, on which I relied heavily for my account of Junkanoo between 1950 and 1980, and for his various other observations about the festival.

The Ministry of Youth and the National Junkanoo Committee, both of which gave me working experience with the Junkanoo parades and allowed me to approach my task with some authority. In addition, the Ministry allowed me the latitude to pursue the work and approved two leaves of absence, during which I was able to work on the book. I am also indebted to the various chairmen of the Junkanoo Committee between 1986 and 1990, particularly Eugene Higgs for securing my appointment to the Committee, and George Bethell, for keeping me there.

Tinkle Hanna, who has been for four years my inspiration, support and friend. During his tenure as Junkanoo Chairman, he devoted himself to the positive development of the festival and approached the parade with the same commitment he reserves for the most important things; in this he demonstrated, through his actions, its value.

All the participants in Junkanoo who have, by their chance remarks or deliberate comments, influenced my vision of this project.

Winston Saunders, for his critical faculties and his constant encouragement, and Philip Burrows, for his clarity of vision.

Last, my family: my brother, Eddie, and cousin, Adrian, for their commitment to the preservation and development of traditional Junkanoo music, and their continued involvement in the festival. My aunt, Eunice, for her critical eye and the use of her home, typewriter and good sense, and for making the initial contact with Macmillan. My grandmothers, for their observations of Nassau in the past; and Peter Ramsay, for his photographs.

Finally, my mother, for her support, in every aspect, of this book; and, especially, my father — for having lived.

For my father
1938 – 1987

Yet, even now, weeks afterwards, I have a very clear mental picture of the queerest Christmas I ever spent . . . and in my ear still runs the monotonous unending rhythm beaten out upon their drums, trumpets and cowbells . . .

(From Amelia Defries, *In a Forgotten Colony,* 1917)

'Cowbells. You know, it's an extraordinary thing . . . when I was abroad I was talking to some friends, and I said, 'You know, the one thing that sends me into ecstasy, even now, in my old age, is the sound of a cowbell on a December night.' And they thought I was crazy. But you know, it was Christmas! . . . the whole sound of Christmas. When they started practice, you know, you could hear . . . And I said, ''On a damp still night, if you heard a cowbell, . . . (even now, it gives me a thrill)'' . . . and they were surprised to hear it because it couldn't mean anything to them at all . . . but to me it meant Christmas . . . just to hear one cowbell . . .'

(Bahamian informant, female, white, septuagenarian. Nassau, December, 1976.)

'Stop Junkanoo?! Man, dey couldn't stop dat! Uh-uh!'

(Bahamian informant, male, black, octogenarian. Nassau, December, 1976.)

Introduction

In 1975, my father was awarded a scholarship to study ethnomusicology at the University of California at Los Angeles. He spent the next two years conducting the first thorough investigation of Bahamian music ever made. In 1978, he submitted his thesis, ''Music in The Bahamas: its Roots, Development and Personality,'' and was awarded a Master's degree. The thesis was comprehensive, examining the religious and secular music indigenous to The Bahamas, and in the final chapters it addressed that practice which has come to be regarded as the cornerstone of Bahamian culture — the Festival of Junkanoo.

How did the last two chapters of an unpublished scholarly work become a book about Junkanoo? At various times after my father's return to Nassau in 1978, he was approached by publishers interested in turning the thesis into a book, and he welcomed the idea. The question was, when was he going to find time to edit it? He was by then the Chief Cultural Affairs Officer in a rapidly developing nation, fully committed to the vision of a Bahamian cultural explosion. The Bahamas had been independent only since 1973, and still had a long way to go before becoming comfortable with its indigenous cultural heritage.

As the main government official charged with the development of culture, my father encouraged artists, persuaded cabinet ministers of the worth of cultural development, and oversaw the entry of The Bahamas into the international sphere. He put together contingents of performers and artists to take part in the Carifestas of 1979 – 82, conducted his choir, the Nassau Renaissance Singers, and oversaw the revival of *Sammie Swain*, the folk opera/ballet he had written in 1968. My father's career culminated in a performance of *Sammie Swain* for Queen Elizabeth II at the time of the Commonwealth Heads of Government Meeting in 1985. Sadly, after this Command Performance his health deteriorated. He died in August 1987 at the age of 49 after a long fight against an hereditary kidney complaint.

My father was a man of vision and had many dreams. This book was only a small dream; while he lived, his goals for the nation were boundless. Nevertheless, it is worthy of fulfillment. And because it is a small dream, it is the one I felt most capable of tackling.

That is not to say that the editing of my father's thesis was a small task. It was, in fact, much more time-consuming than I had anticipated; the ten years it had lain untouched had seen major developments in almost every aspect of Junkanoo, and my father's comments in 1977 on the 'modern' days barely foreshadowed the changes which were to come. It is largely for this reason that this book deals only generally with what I call Modern Junkanoo. It focusses more on the development of Junkanoo up to the late 1940s than on its growth since then.

Like my father, I have chosen to approach the festival from

its relation to the social development of The Bahamas and in this regard, the period up to 1953 is far more heavily documented than the years following. Perhaps that is because the chroniclers of Bahamian history have all been able to remember the fifties, sixties and seventies in the Bahamas, and have therefore been concerned with the preservation of information about years gone by. Perhaps it is because they feel, as I do when faced with the task of writing about people I have met, that they are not sufficiently distant from the events of recent years to write objectively about them. Those are the years my father emphasised; it was with some surprise that I discovered that the years from 1948 to 1977 account for only three-and-a-half pages of his manuscript.

Developments in Junkanoo since the 1940s have been highly complex. Until then Junkanoo was predominantly a pastime of working-class blacks; middle-class Bahamians, no matter what their colour, together with upper-class whites, had very little to do with the event. However, the 1950s saw the first substantial participation of young coloured middle-class Bahamians in the parade, and during the following decades, Junkanoo came more and more to be their domain. These days, indeed, every major group is headed by a caucus of middle-class Bahamians — doctors, lawyers, architects, civil servants, artists, accountants and educators; those junkanoos who still hold fast to their working-class roots tend to be individual competitors, or young men trying to break into the winning monopoly of the major Junkanoo groups. It would be easy to say that the attainment of majority rule in 1967 and the subsequent legitimising of the parades are solely responsible for this change; but it is my belief that the foundations for

this phenomenon were laid as early as the 1940s and 1950s. Exactly what those foundations were, and how they were developed, are the stuff of further research. As my task has been the editing and expansion of my father's work and not the collection of fresh data, I have decided to put that work off until a later date.

The festival of Junkanoo is a symbolic occasion in more ways than one. For years, it represented the temporary freedom of the black Bahamian to dance, sing and make 'noise' on Bay Street, the very heart of the whites' power. Since the organisation and subsequent victory of the black voters, however, that aspect of its symbolism has been lost — as evidenced by the recent unpopular proposal to shift the site of the annual parades from Bay Street to the Queen Elizabeth Sports Centre. For years, too, Junkanoo has provided links with the Bahamian's unique African heritage; its very survival has indicated that the Bahamian celebration cannot be viewed as being simply an offshoot of the more well-researched Jamaican John Canoe. In this regard, then, Junkanoo may be viewed as a public symbol of the Bahamian's Africanness, and may provide clues to the meaning of other Caribbean festivals, rather than vice versa.

In recent years, however, it seems that Junkanoo, while growing in beauty and cost, has been losing its distinctive character. The development of tourism and the zeal for cultural advancement have resulted in an imposition of numerous rules on the parade, and have thus led to its distancing from the ordinary Bahamian. More and more, Junkanoo is becoming a spectacle, a show in which only the few can take part; more and more, it is becoming a commodity to be mass-produced and sold to audiences. At the same time, and for a variety of reasons, Bahamian schoolchildren have been growing unsure of their heritage; they appear as ready to identify with Jamaica and the United States as they are with their own country. To

Music and Dance (Mr and Mrs N. Klonaris, Lyford Cay, Nassau)

Young Music Maker (private collection)

chronicle the history, development and meaning of the festival has therefore become important.

What I have added to my father's thesis is based on certain historical and social information which has become available since 1977. When my father undertook his research, there were only two comprehensive histories of his country: Michael Craton's *History of The Bahamas*, first published in 1962 and updated in 1968 after the PLP came to power, and Dr Paul Albury's *Story of The Bahamas*, published in 1975. Since that time, several major historical works have been produced including a 1986 revision of the Craton text; most important among them were Gail Saunders' various published and unpublished studies. Since that time, too, Junkanoo has been the subject of at least one PhD dissertation, Keith Wisdom's *Bahamian Junkanoo: An Act in a Modern Social Drama* (1985), which I found especially helpful for my summary of Junkanoo's later years. What I have done, then, is to add the new information to the old, in the hope of creating an interesting, readable account of the development of Bahamian Junkanoo.

In the conclusion to his thesis, my father wrote:

> What then of the future? . . . Will The Bahamas, in its pursuit of progress, reject its rich cultural heritage and succumb to the powerful cultural influences of its nearest neighbour, the North American technological giant? As citizens of a newly independent nation, Bahamians alone can decide these questions. In the words of Sylvia Winter, the Jamaican sociologist, ''if we are to become conscious of ourselves as a people, as an entity, then we must confront ourselves with our origins, must lay claim to and take hold of our history,'' for it is only by so doing, that the future of a music distinctly Bahamian can be ensured.

Wise words. It is for this reason above all that I offer this little bit of our history; I hope that as Bahamians, we will take a firm hold of it.

1
Junkanoo and The Bahamas
An Overview

Twice every year, on Boxing and New Year's Days, thousands of people throng Nassau's main thoroughfare to witness the parade known as Junkanoo. In front of them, rival groups of dancers and drummers vie for the glory which comes from winning the parade: they carry fantastic costumes under the street lights to the rhythm of cowbells and drums, each group trying to better the others in beauty of costume, fineness of music, and excellence of performance. Later, after the sun has risen and competitors and watchers alike have begun to wilt, a winner is announced. And that, for many, will be the news of the week; Christmas, for Bahamians, is Junkanoo.

It was not always so. At times the festival was viewed favorably by the government; at others, however, it was threatened with extinction. Whenever The Bahamas was prosperous and the Bahamian people content, Junkanoo was accepted and even encouraged. When, on the other hand, the islands were beset with hardship, the parades were suppressed. A study of the development of Junkanoo, therefore, provides us with valuable insight into the social, political, economic and cultural development of the nation.

In order fully to understand the place of the festival in Bahamian life, it is necessary first to have some idea of the nature and history both of the islands, and of the festival itself. This chapter therefore looks at the history of the islands and the roots of Junkanoo.

The Islands

Extending along the edge of the Atlantic Ocean for some 600 miles between the south eastern coast of Florida and the northern coast of Haiti lies The Bahamas, an archipelago of approximately 700 islands and over 2,000 rocks and cays. The origin of the name is unclear, but it very possibly lies in the Lucayan *Buhama*. For many years it was thought that the name derived from the Spanish *baja mar*, 'shallow sea', but in fact the Spaniards called the islands *Lucayos* as early as 1500, and even up to the present time some Spanish maps still use the name. The islands have an estimated total land mass of 5,382 square miles, somewhat more than that of Jamaica, and the surrounding waters abound in reefs, shoals, banks and channels of great natural beauty and account for four-fifths of the country's area.

The islands, which are formed of coral limestone, are low and flat. The highest point is Mount Alvernia, a 206-foot-high hill located on Cat Island, at the centre of the chain. With the exception of the more well developed settlements, where luxuriant tropical vegetation flourishes, the terrain is characterised by sparse pine forests in the north, and by low-lying shrubs, brackish lakes and mangrove swamps in the south. Thin layers of fertile soil are found in pockets in the porous limestone rock, which makes farming a hard business. Despite

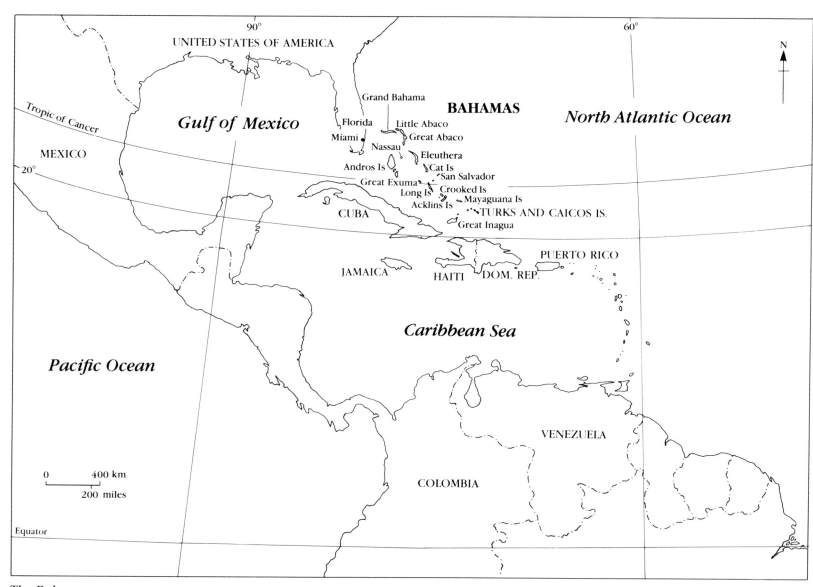

UNITED STATES OF AMERICA

BAHAMAS

Gulf of Mexico

North Atlantic Ocean

Tropic of Cancer

90°

60°

N

Grand Bahama

Florida

Little Abaco

Miami

Great Abaco

Nassau

MEXICO

Eleuthera

20°

Andros Is

Cat Is

San Salvador

Great Exuma

Crooked Is

Long Is

Mayaguana Is

Acklins Is

TURKS AND CAICOS IS.

CUBA

Great Inagua

JAMAICA

HAITI

DOM. REP.

PUERTO RICO

Caribbean Sea

Pacific Ocean

VENEZUELA

0   400 km

200 miles

COLOMBIA

Equator

The Bahamas

this somewhat harsh landscape, The Bahamas boasts one of the most equable climates in the world with few temperatures below 60°F in winter or above 90°F in summer.

Over twenty of the islands are inhabited, most of the 250,000 people (population projection, *1990 Bahamas Handbook*) are centred in two cities — Nassau, the capital, on New Providence, and Freeport, on Grand Bahama. The other islands, in the past known as Out Islands and now called Family Islands, continue to be sparsely populated as more and more islanders move to the urban areas.

The History

The Bahamas has rightly been called the 'Gateway to the New World', for it was on the Bahamian island of Guanahani, traditionally identified as the present-day San Salvador, that Christopher Columbus first landed after the historic Atlantic crossing of 1492. Here, as in the islands adjacent, he found a simple, peace-loving people, beautiful in body and generous of heart. They called themselves *Lukku-cairi*, 'island people'.

These Lucayans, as they later came to be known, were related to the Arawaks then resident in the larger Caribbean islands, and were directly descended from the Taino of Hispaniola. The Arawaks had centuries before migrated northwards through the islands of the Caribbean Sea from their place of origin in South America. It is likely that the Bahama Islands were populated before their arrival by the Siboney, a group of Indians connected with tribes of the North American mainland, and the Lucayans who met Columbus were, in all probability, descended from both Siboney and Arawak stock. At the time of the Spaniards' landfall there were between twenty and thirty thousand of them scattered throughout the Bahamas, a peaceful and simple people. But neither the Lucayans nor their islands held much attraction for the Spaniards, who, in their quest for gold, quickly moved south towards the Greater Antilles. It was only after their gold mines and plantations had been established in Hispaniola that the Spaniards looked to The Bahamas as a source of labour.

The guileless Lucayans were no match for the Spaniards. Within twenty-five years all but a few had been captured and taken to Hispaniola, and there they succumbed under the harsh régime of enforced labour in the mines. Peter Martyr, a contemporary writer, described their fate in 1511.

> The Lucayans, torn from their homes, became perfectly desperate. Some have died from exhaustion, refusing all food and hiding themselves in inaccessible valleys, deserted forests, and unknown mountain heights; while others have put an end to their unendurable lives. Those of more hopeful temperament clung to life, in the hope of one day regaining their freedom. The majority of those who were able to escape, betook themselves to the northern parts of Hispaniola, where they might breathe the air wafted from their native country; with extended arms and open mouths they seemed to drink with their native air, and when misery reduced them to exhaustion, they dropped dead upon the ground.

> (From *De Orbo Novo*, trans. F.A. McNutt, 1912.)

In fairness to the Spaniards, in 1516 they appointed Bartolome de Las Casas 'Protector of the Indians'. At his instigation a search throughout The Bahamas was undertaken in an effort to collect the remaining Lucayans and resettle them as free inhabitants in Hispaniola. After three years of searching, however, only eleven persons had been found; their removal constituted the last documented activity of the Lucayan people.

The Bahamas, though at first technically part of the Spanish domain, was ignored by the Europeans for almost 130 years. In 1629 Charles I of England, in laying formal claim to the

Carolinas, arbitrarily included The Bahamas, but there was no immediate settlement of the islands as a result. It was not until 1648, when Dissenters, Independents and Puritans fled from religious persecution in Bermuda and England, that the first English settlements were established. The early settlers, led by Captain William Sayle, called themselves 'Eleutherian Adventurers' — from the Greek word *Eleutheria*, or 'freedom' — and gave the name Eleuthera to the island on which they landed. From here the inhabitants quickly spread to Spanish Wells, Harbour Island, and, possibly, New Providence.

Soon after the colony was established, it became the repository for free blacks, recalcitrant slaves and whites banished from Bermuda, which was then considered overpopulated. Life in the fledgling Bahamian colony was fraught with hardships and the Adventurers barely managed to eke out a meagre living from farming the land.

Sometime before 1666, Bermudian seamen became attracted to other Bahamian islands because of the salt, ambergris and spoils from Spanish wrecks to be found there. New Providence was officially inhabited around this time, and Charles Town, the main settlement, established. Its population was further augmented by certain farming families and slaves from Bermuda, and by 1671 the population of the entire Bahamas was estimated at 1,097, about 40 per cent of whom were slaves.

The islands at this time had no form of organised local government, and therefore King Charles II officially granted them to the Lords Proprietors of the Carolinas, who appointed a series of governors to look after their interests in the colony. As these Proprietors were little more than absentee landlords, this form of government proved to be ineffectual, and the inhabitants, soon disenchanted with the agricultural limitations of the soil, gave themselves over to the more lucrative occupation of plundering the treasure-laden Spanish and French ships

History of Junkanoo (Mr O. Bodie Jr, Nassau)

passing through Bahamian waters en route for Europe. In retaliation, New Providence was sacked by Spanish forces from Cuba in 1684.

For the next 30 years, the islands became the rendez-vous for privateers, buccaneers and pirates, the most notorious of whom were Edward 'Blackbeard' Teach, and two female pirates, Ann Bonney and Mary Read. During the War of the Spanish Succession, New Providence was again attacked by joint Spanish and French forces and Charles Town burnt to the ground. Many families moved to Cat Island, Exuma and Harbour Island. A second settlement of New Providence was not attempted until 1687, this time with immigrants from Jamaica. The town was rebuilt in 1694 and the name changed to Nassau, in honour of William III, Prince of Orange-Nassau. The pirates, meanwhile, had continued to use New Providence as their headquarters and to all intents and purposes The Bahamas had become a 'Pirates' Republic'.

By 1717 the situation had so deteriorated that King George I felt compelled to dispatch Captain Woodes Rogers, a naval officer and former privateer, accompanied by four warships of the Royal Navy, to restore law and order in the islands. Rogers, a man of courage and determination, routed the pirates, hanging many in public and deporting others. In 1718 Rogers was appointed Captain-General and Governor-in-Chief of the Bahama Islands, and he ruled the colony, strongly opposed by many settlers, for the next three years. In 1721, however, most of his supporters died in an epidemic and he was forced to leave The Bahamas for England, where, since he had spent most of his money on re-ordering the colony, he spent years in gaol for debt. Eight years later, Rogers was re-appointed Governor of The Bahamas, and in 1729 the colony was granted an elective form of government under a Royal Governor. The former Bahamian motto, *Expulsis Piratis Restituta Commercia* (Pirates Expelled, Commerce Restored),

dates from this time.

During the peaceful years which followed, close relationships between The Bahamas and the mainland American colonies developed. Trade was encouraged and there was a considerable market for Bahamian salt and hardwoods. Travel was frequent between the islands and the coastal colonies, particularly the Carolinas, and it was not uncommon for an ex-governor from the mainland to be sent to The Bahamas.

These ties, however, were abruptly shattered at the beginning of the American War of Independence. In 1776, Nassau was invaded by the Americans and occupied for 15 days. The Spanish also took this opportunity to attack in 1781, their occupation lasting until 1783, when by the Treaty of Versailles, the islands were returned to England.

But the Declaration of Independence was to have far-reaching effects: thousands of American colonists who were loyal to the Crown sought refuge in the Bahamas. The first arrivals came from New York in 1783 and settled in Abaco, but the majority came with their remaining property and slaves from the Carolinas, Georgia, and, later, Florida. With a view to growing cotton, they established sizable plantations throughout the archipelago and settled, among others, the islands of New Providence, Abaco, Andros, Long Island, Cat Island and Exuma. In order to facilitate these Loyalists, King George III bought all rights from the original Lords Proprietors and granted to each immigrant head of family 40 acres of land without tax for ten years.

Population figures soared. In 1783, when the first Loyalists landed, the population had been roughly 4,050, of which 2,330 (58%) were black. By 1789, when the last newcomers had arrived, the population was 11,300, of whom 8,000 (71%) were black. The early cotton crops were successful and the economy of the islands benefitted tremendously. In 1773 and 1774 exports to Britain were valued at £5,000; in 1786 and

1787 their value was £59,000. In addition, real estate prices rose, and it seemed that The Bahamas was at last well on the road to prosperity.

But the cotton industry would flourish for fewer than twenty years. Thin soil, primitive farming techniques, parasites and the burgeoning American cotton industry all took their toll. By the turn of the century, the plantations had failed. Many of the Loyalists, disheartened, left the Out Islands. Some departed the colony altogether; others, abandoning their plantations and their slaves, chose to settle in Nassau. Still others, too poor to give up their investments, stayed on their land, diversifying their produce, attaining some level of self-sufficiency, and creating communities which were, for all practical purposes, independent of the capital. Their presence in the islands, however, left a legacy which would change the face of the colony. Their numbers and their relative sophistication (several had come from American cities) helped to modernise Bahamian society, and they had provided some contact with events in the outside world. Thanks to them, too, the number of blacks in The Bahamas had grown, in the space of a decade, from just under three-fifths of the entire population to almost three-quarters; and many of the Out Islands were now settled predominantly by slaves.

The Bahamian slaves came mainly from coastal areas of West Africa and the Congo and among them were represented the Mandingo, Fulani, Hausa, Ibo, Ijo, Yoruba, Ashanti and Congo peoples. Slavery in The Bahamas was rather different from that in the rest of the West Indies. The Bahamas would never be a sugar-producing colony; for the bulk of the population, the land was only a secondary source of livelihood. Any hopes to create a plantation economy in The Bahamas were short-lived at best.

Even when the cotton industry was at its height, then, plantation life in The Bahamas differed from that found elsewhere in the New World. Estates were, for the most part, relatively small, and there were few great plantation houses to maintain. Even where a plantation occupied a large tract of land, only small portions could be cultivated at a time; as a result, very few Loyalists owned more than a hundred slaves, and these tended to be employed in teams of about a dozen at a time. Most often the planter himself supervised their work so that there was no need for the paid overseer, whose job depended on the output of the slaves. Moreover, most slave owners in The Bahamas employed the 'task system' of labour: each slave was apportioned a certain daily quota of work, and when that had been completed, he was technically free to do as he pleased. There was one respect, however, in which the lives of the Bahamian slaves were similar to those of their brothers elsewhere; they were traditionally given three days off at Christmas — a fact which would encourage the development of Bahamian Junkanoo.

In 1807 free blacks were permitted to vote, and when the Emancipation Act was proclaimed in 1834, there were already four 'men of colour' sitting in the Bahamian House of Assembly. Although the Act made all slaves in the British possessions technically free, a period of four years' apprenticeship was applied, after which the freed slaves were left on their own. As a result many of the blacks, particularly in the Out Islands, were abandoned to poverty.

In addition to those already there, The Bahamas continued to receive Free Africans until 1860. These were the human cargoes of illegal slavers captured on the high seas by the ships of the Royal Navy. Freed immediately on arrival in The Bahamas, they settled in the Out Islands and on New Providence, where they were sent to the villages of Grant's Town, Carmichael and Adelaide, all specially designed for this purpose.

The archipelago also provided the ideal refuge for American runaways, who settled in the various islands until their emanci-

Junkanoo Profile (Mr C. Blackwell, Jamaica)

officially neutral, became the vital trading link between England and the South. The normally peaceful city suddenly became the hub of trading activity, and money flowed. In 1860, imports were valued at £234,029 and exports £157,350; by 1864 they were valued at £5,346,112 and £4,672,398 respectively. J.H. Stark, a nineteenth-century historian, paints a graphic picture of Nassau during this period.

> Everyone was mad with excitement during these years of the war. The shops were packed to the ceilings, the streets were crowded with bales, boxes and barrels. Fortunes were made in a few weeks or months. Money was spent and scattered in a most extravagant and lavish manner. The town actually swarmed with Southern refugees, captains and crews of blockade-runners. Every available space in or out of doors was occupied. Men lay on verandahs, walls, decks and floors. Money was plentiful and sailors sometimes landed with $1,500 in specie. Wages were doubled, liquor flowed freely and the common labourer had his champagne and rich food. Not since the days of the buccaneers and pirates had there been such times in The Bahamas.

> (From J.H. Stark, *History and Guide to The Bahamas*, 1891.)

Charleston, South Carolina, and Wilmington, North Carolina, were two of the busiest southern ports during the blockade. It is noteworthy that marked similarities in speech patterns and dialect between the inhabitants of North Carolina and the Bahamas prevail to the present day. Of interest also is the fact that Wilmington was the chief scene of *John Kuner* revels during the latter part of the 19th century, celebrations which resembled the traditional Bahamian Junkanoo parades.

When the war ended in 1865, however, The Bahamas slipped back into economic depression. To make matters worse, in the following year the islands were struck by one of the most devastating hurricanes in their history. From 1865 to 1920

pation in 1863. By that time, the American Civil War had brought The Bahamas unexpected prosperity. In 1861, President Lincoln had proclaimed a sea blockade of all Southern ports, and the South, needing war supplies and an outlet for its cotton, appealed to Britain for aid. Nassau, many Bahamian labourers were forced to seek work in the United States, Cuba and Central America, while the chief occupations of those who elected to remain at home were the production of pineapples, citrus fruit, sponges and sisal.

A degree of prosperity was experienced in the south-eastern islands due to the salt industry in Inagua. In addition, the development of Central America provided much needed employment for Bahamians. Matthew Town, Inagua, became an important port of call for German and Dutch ships en route to Central America and it was from here that Bahamian contract labourers left to work in Panama, Mexico, Guatemala and Nicaragua.

When war broke out in 1914, the colony was hardly affected. After the entry of the USA into the War in 1917, however, the poverty which had plagued The Bahamas for the past fifty years intensified. Armistice did little to ease the situation; the islands remained bitterly poor until 1920.

In 1919, the United States Congress passed the Volstead Act, which made it a federal offence to manufacture, sell, transport, export or import liquor. The Act came into effect in early 1920, and provided The Bahamas at last with a means of making money. By supplying the thirsty Americans with illegal liquor during the Prohibition period (1920 – 1933), many Bahamian merchants were able to amass considerable wealth.

Prohibition came to an end in 1933, however, with the inauguration of Franklin D. Roosevelt. One of his first deeds was the repealing of the Volstead Act, with the result that The Bahamas, hitherto only slightly affected by the Depression, was plunged once more into poverty. The two decades following were again lean years for The Bahamas. Some relief was provided during the 1940s by work on war-related projects in New Providence and the United States, but it was not until the 1950s, when the government decided to exploit the tourist and real estate markets to their fullest, that the economy was revitalised.

This period also saw the awakening of political awareness among Bahamian blacks. Economic and political control of the country had previously rested in the hands of a small minority of established white Bahamian families. Since the 1930s, however, the black labouring population had been expressing its dissatisfaction with the state of affairs in various protests, the most important of them being the Burma Road Riot of 1942. In 1953, the first Bahamian political party was established. Dubbed the Progressive Liberal Party, its members were drawn from the growing black middle class, and its mandate was the representation of the predominantly black majority. By 1956 the P.L.P. had provoked the white members of the government to form their own political alliance, the United Bahamian Party, which it opposed in the General Elections of that year. Although it lost, the P.L.P.'s efforts ultimately provoked several long-awaited electoral reforms, including the introduction of the secret ballot, women's suffrage, and one vote per head. In 1958, the P.L.P. and the newly-formed Labour Party supported a general strike which lasted for nineteen days; in 1962 women voted for the first time; and in 1967 the P.L.P. won the general election and formed the government. Independence was granted to the colony in 1973, and The Bahamas became a sovereign nation within the British Commonwealth.

The People

By 1860 most of the social factors which have had a major influence on the present structure of Bahamian society had been implanted. Subsequently, the migratory movements of peoples, the resulting fusion of cultural concepts, the physical conditions of life and the availability of natural resources have all contributed to the evolution of a distinct 'personality' of the Bahamian people.

Although the indigenous inhabitants were the Lucayan Indians, the majority (85%) of the present-day Bahamians are of West African origin mixed with some European blood; the remainder are the white descendants of Anglo-Saxon colonisers and American Loyalists.

While fishing, farming and ship building remain the chief sources of livelihood for the Out Islanders, tourism and banking together account for the bulk of the Bahamian economy, one of the healthiest in the region. Tourism generates as much as fifty per cent of the gross national product, and is responsible for the employment, directly or indirectly, of roughly half the working population. During the 1980s, visitor arrivals rose to over three million per year, and in 1988, tourist expenditure had climbed to $1.14 billion. Offshore banking contributes to about eight per cent of the gross national product, employing approximately 3,000 people and spending roughly $240 million in The Bahamas. The Bahamian standard of living is thus relatively high, with per capita incomes among the highest in the area; however, as almost every commodity is imported, the cost of living is similarly high. (All statistics from *1990 Bahamas Handbook*.)

The Bahamas today represents a rich fusion of many different elements. The result of miscegenation between the Africans and early Europeans is evident throughout the islands and the texture of the society has been further enriched by the influx, during the early part of the present century, of Greek sponge merchants, Cantonese and Semitic businessmen, West Indian professionals and skilled workers, and Haitian labourers.

Independent since 1973, The Bahamas has inherited its language, religion, and systems of education and government from Britain. Owing to its proximity to the United States, its life-style has become increasingly North American in recent years; nevertheless, many manifestations in the socio-cultural life of its people still reflect West African roots.

Lodges and burial societies dating back to the mid-nineteenth century, for example, proliferate throughout the islands. Originally established as 'Friendly Societies' to provide the poorer inhabitants of the community with financial support, they ensured that their members would receive sickness benefits and — most important — decent funerals. Their original names, such as the Congo United Society (founded 1864), and the Ibo, Fulani, Hausa and Yoruba Societies, point both to the West African tribal origins of the earlier black Bahamians and the very African nature of the organisations. However, many of these names have since been changed, or the societies themselves absorbed into larger American-based Lodges, and few tribal distinctions have been retained.

The Yoruba credit institution known as *esu* or *esusu* also has an exact parallel in The Bahamas, where it is known as *a-sue*. *Esusu* is the clubbing together of money by various people in order to save up a lump sum over a fixed period of time. A set amount is agreed upon, and each contributor pays it to a president at a regular place and time. Usually the sum is submitted weekly, but it is not uncommon in The Bahamas to find monthly a-sues as well. The president then pays the entire amount to each member in turn, thus enabling them to collect sizable sums of money at set times of the month or year. In The Bahamas the 'president' is merely referred to as the person who 'holds the a-sue'; the fixed sum is called a 'hand', and persons contributing are said to be 't'rowing a hand'. This system is widely practised throughout the islands.

Another surviving Africanism in The Bahamas is the practice of *obeah*, a phenomenon of the supernatural which has the power to influence individuals for good or evil, to cause and cure either physical or mental illness, and generally to provide solutions to the attendant problems of everyday life. The chief practitioner of the art is the local Obeah man or Obeah woman who uses all manner of aids — medicinal herbs, fetishes, incantations — to achieve the desired results.

It is perhaps in the area of music and dance, however, that connecting links with both West Africa and Europe may best be observed. Many of the folk songs and ballads owe much to a European heritage; the quadrille dances still performed in certain Family Islands are examples of a perfect union of the two cultures; and it is likely that the Junkanoo festival originated in Africa.

Roots of Junkanoo

Where the name **Junkanoo** comes from is unclear. For some contemporary Junkanoo leaders, for instance, its meaning is contained in the word 'junk'. For years costumes and instruments were created from cast-off items — drums were made from old barrels, bells from scrap metal, and costumes from anything available. The early junkanoo participants were skilled at taking such 'junk' materials and forging them anew, turning them into works of beauty.

The goombay drum of Junkanoo is constructed from a wooden or metal barrel, originally the container of food, rum or oil, and has a single membrane of sheep or goat skin stretched and nailed over one end; the other is left open. These drums are often decorated with stripes, geometric designs or glass fragments, bottle caps, and even coloured lights. The drum is carried under one arm, supported by a strap which runs over the opposite shoulder, and is played with the bare hands. The other important Junkanoo instrument is the cowbell, a flat-sided clapper bell. They range in size from six to fourteen inches long, and are usually played in pairs. They

Scrap gang (Cisalpine Overseas Bank)

are joined by a cord or chain, held one in each hand, and shaken or struck together. When they are played singly, they are held in both hands and shaken.

It is almost certain, too, that the Bahamian Junkanoo festival is related to the *John Canoe* revels held elsewhere in the New World; the etymology of that name has engaged researchers for centuries. Both Edward Long (*History of Jamaica*, London, 1774) and W. J. Gardner (*History of Jamaica*, New York, 1909) suggest that the festival is connected with the memory of a West African headman named John Connu or Conny. Noted for his economic and political power in the Gold Coast during the eighteenth century, this leader commanded the Brandenburg trading fort in Axim in the early 1770s, and dealt, among other things, in slaves.

The Ghanaian writer K. Y. Daaku, author of *Trade and Politics on the Gold Coast 1600 – 1720* (1970), devotes a chapter of that work to "the Merchant Princes — John Kabes and John Konny". Of the latter he writes:

> A contemporary of John Kabes who was economically, socially and politically as powerful was John Konny (Kounie, Kony) of Pokoso, Ahanta. A man of strong personality and character, he ignored Dutch threats, openly defied them, and successfully pitted his power against an Anglo-Dutch alliance in 1711. For almost fifteen years he baffled the calculations of the Dutch ruler with connections reaching as far inland as Asante. His attempts to inject life into the Brandenburg African Company won enthusiastic acclaim in Germany. For his efforts, he won for himself the appellation 'the last Prussian Negro Prince'. He faithfully supported a flag the limits of whose power he could neither know nor visualise. His stout defence of the former Brandenburg possessions resulted in the headquarters at Pokoso being known as 'Connie's Castle', even after he had been driven away by the Dutch.

It is generally accepted, thanks to records of the slave traffic between West Africa and the New World Territories, that the planters in the British colonies, particularly Jamaica, preferred slaves chosen from the Ashanti-Fanti peoples of the Gold Coast. The French, on the other hand, favoured Dahomeans and their allied tribes, and the Iberians the Yoruba of Western Nigeria. If the name *John Canoe* is indeed derived from the caboceer (A *Caboceer* was the headman of a West African tribe) John Conny of the Gold Coast, this would explain why the term is only found among former British possessions —

Jamaica, Belize, North Carolina and The Bahamas. What is more, the early records of the festival indicate that the John Canoe masks, so often described as 'grotesque', were designed to frighten viewers, particularly children; and as it is difficult to believe that the early slaves would have remembered John Conny with anything but fear, the theory is further strengthened. Finally, it is possible that several Africans in the British West Indies were obtained directly from Conny's Castle. If this were in fact the case, is it any wonder that the John Canoe they depicted was a figure of terror?

Certain arguments, however, have been advanced for a French origin for the name. These stem from the traditional association of John Canoe with St Vincent, the one island in the John Canoe group which has any French connections. Three possible words stand out: *jongleur*, after European mediaeval bards; *gens inconnus*, suggested by the masks worn, and *jeunes canneurs*, after the young cane-cutters on the sugar plantations. Attractive as they might seem, it is difficult for any of these suggested origins to hold water. The last, for instance, must be discarded simply because, of the four territories where the name John Canoe is used, two — The Bahamas and North Carolina — were never producers of sugar. The other two seem plausible enough until we realise that in St Vincent the name *John Canoe* was not used for the Christmas festivities at all. The figure known elsewhere as John Canoe was called by the Vincentians the *Moco Jumbo*. It would perhaps be more accurate to look to the African settlers on Bequia, an island off the coast of St Vincent, for inspiration; for they were the maroon descendants of Mocos who had been shipwrecked there. It was they, and not the French-speaking Vincentians, who called their celebrations John Canoe.

The theory that the term stems from two Hebrew words, *Jona* (a dove) and *caken* (sacred), advanced in 1826 by the traveller C.R. Williams, is too remote to be taken seriously, despite the fact that the house carried on the head of the Jamaican John Canoe was believed to be an emblem of Noah's Ark. Similarly, there is no historical evidence to support the suggestion that the term is derived from *janquannu* a Mayan procession of masked singers, dancers and musicians, though there is a strong phonetic likeness between the two terms.

In 1777, Charles Middleton, author of the book *A New and Complete System of Geography*, noted that a West African tribe called the Quojas:

> believe in one supreme being though they cannot form any just idea of him. They call him *Canno*, and attributed to him are infinite power, and universal knowledge, and suppose him to be present everywhere. They also believe that the dead become spirits whom they call *Jannanin*, that is, patrons or defenders, and suppose them able to protect them in all calamities . . . though they appear to pay great reverence to Canno, yet their religious worship is chiefly directed to these spirits whom they daily invoke.

Two hundred years later, in a 1942 article entitled "The John Canoe Festival, A New World Africanism", the cultural anthropologist Ira de A. Reid postulated that the names *Jannanin* and *Canno* may have in some way been associated with John Canoe. For him, and for certain others, the festival thus had some religious significance. Nevertheless, however attractive the theory that John Canoe was the relic of some deeply religious African ritual, it must be discounted for the following reason: of all the institutions upheld by the Africans in the New World, those which were considered most sacred (gods and religion, the reverence of ancestral spirits, the knowledge of herbs and medicine) were never flaunted before profane eyes. On the contrary, these institutions were protected from outsiders and shrouded in secrecy. Needless to say, the eyes of the European masters were most emphatically profane.

It is no coincidence that the Haitian reverence of *loa* (divinities) has for many years been confused (by Westerners) with a parallel worship of Catholic saints. Nor is it accidental that the most powerful slave practices throughout the New World (such as the extensive use of herbs and poisons, the gatherings of Voudou/Shango acolytes, the rituals of Obeah practitioners) were, and are to this day, carried out in secret. In The Bahamas alone, we need look no further than the Bahamian ring dances — the Fire Dance and the Jumping Dance — for examples of rituals which were routinely hidden from masters. The New World Africans were painfully aware of their vulnerability. Consequently, they allowed their masters no hold on the source of their inner strength — religion, sorcery, herbal lore, the knowledge of the true names of things. What they considered most powerful was what they most perfectly concealed.

It may, of course, be argued that, for the African, religion is inextricably bound to the process of day-to-day living. One researcher, Deidrich Westermann, has done just that. In Africa, he states,

> religion is not a sphere separate from, or transcending, the rest of life's activities; rather does it stand on the same level with these, working through the same agencies and striving for the same ends as all other activities. The African's world of being does not separate itself into a sacred and profane realm.

> (From *Die Kpelle, ein Negerstaum en Liberia,* 1921.)

While this may be true in Africa, it must also be acknowledged that the Africans in the New World were forced to observe a strict set of hierarchical values, religious and otherwise. To be a slave was to be sub-human; a slave was

Dreams of Africa or Junkanoo Warrior, now destroyed
(Mr and Mrs R. Lightbourne, Nassau)

uniqueness of slavery ... lay in the fact that the labourer himself was a commodity, not merely his labour or labour-power. His loss of control, furthermore, extended to the infinity of time, to his children and his children's children.

Africans in the Americas owned nothing: names, spouses and offspring were all the property of their masters. What was more, they were aliens, forced to speak a language which was not their mother tongue and work in foreign lands. What was natural in Africa, therefore, had to be adjusted to fit the slaves' new environment; whatever could not conform to the plantation was discarded or changed. The commonplace thus became the ritual, the open became the secret, and the habitual the ceremonial. If the idea of a hierarchical society was foreign to the native of Africa, it was the law by which the American slaves lived; and as a result, the Africans in the New World made definite distinctions between practices reserved for the initiated and those which could be shared by all. John Canoe, by its very nature, falls into the latter category.

Just as the suggestion of a religious origin of John Canoe must be laid aside, so too must the theory that John Canoe is linked to sorcery. Frederic Cassidy, author of the book *Jamaican Talk*, suggests that the name of the festival could derive from two Ewe words, *dzono* (sorcerer) and *Kono* (something deadly, cause of death). But just as there is no evidence to support the religious argument, so too is there no historical indication that John Canoe was ever associated with witchcraft. Indeed, all the evidence points to the contrary. Those practices which gave the slaves power over their enemies were jealously guarded; those which supported the Europeans' idea of Africans as happy, child-like creatures — a love of singing and dancing, storytelling and drama — were paraded before the planters. Were John Canoe descended from religion or magic, it would have been held in secret.

something owned, someone who was not permitted to possess anything at all. As M.I. Finley, author of *Ancient Slavery and Modern Ideology* (1980), points out:

> The slaveowner's rights over his slave-property were total in more ways than one. The slave, being a slave, suffered ... total loss of control over his person and his personality: the

Of all the theories about the derivation of the festival's name, one stands out as not only possible, but likely. Robert Dirks and Virginia Kerns, authors of a study of the John Canoe parade, published in Belize in 1975, commented:

We find it irresistible to speculate on some resemblances between John Canoe and a dance performed by the Bambara people of West Africa. The Bambara's tribal domain extends into the Ivory Coast region, an area that was heavily slaved by the European powers. Today, the Bambara still conduct traditional agricultural rites in which the premier dance is the *kono* . . . aside from the linguistic similarities, there are two reasons to suspect that the Bambara's *kono* may have served as the model for Jamaica's *Canoe*. In the first place, as an agricultural rite, *kono* shares an affinity with John Canoe, which clearly bore the stamp of a first-fruits ceremony in the early days. Moreover, the *kono*, like the early versions of John Canoe, is performed in animal masquerades.

(From 'John Canoe', in *National Studies*, Vol.3, No.6, 1975.)

The word *Kono* may, in fact, be central to the unravelling of the mystery. One of the aspects of John Canoe, previously overlooked by researchers, is the presence of the stilt dancers. Although little has been written about stilts in West Africa, two monographs by K. G. Lindblom (1927 and 1928) noted a high correlation among stilts, masks and secret societies in the region. According to Lindblom's study, it was the peoples of the coastal regions of north-west Africa (such as Bambara), and not the Ashanti-Fanti peoples, who used masks and stilts. As we know that two of the most pervasive elements in John Canoe, from the earliest observation of the festival, were masks, often with some kind of animal symbolism, and stilts, we may deduce that the slaves' Ashanti-Fanti ancestors had less to do with John Canoe than it might at first seem.

In this connection it is worth noting that a *Kono* Secret Society, listed as a social organisation in Butt-Thompson's *West African Secret Societies*, exists among the people of Sierra Leone, and that the Dan people of Liberia claim that their tradition of stilt dancing is not indigenous but that the origin is *Kono*, to the north of the Dan. Again, the origin of the stilts is attributed not to the people of the central West African coast, but to people further north.

In *The Sociology of Slavery*, Orlando Patterson cited three possible West African recreational activities which may have contributed (the key word here) to the phenomenon of John Canoe. They were: "the yam festival activities of the *Mno* secret society of the *Ibo* peoples; the recreational activities of the *Eguugun* secret society of the *Yoruba*; and the *Homowo* harvest festival of the *Ga* peoples." In the first, masked dancers impersonating ancestral spirits appeared at seasonal periods. In the second, the exclusively male members of the Eguugun secret society masquerade in magnificent masks and costumes in order to invoke the assistance of the ancestral ghosts of the Yoruba in their agricultural activities. In the third, elaborate yam feasts incorporating drinking and dancing in remembrance of the dead are held each year and are followed by a procession led by masked novices of the society. Typical of this procession are "buffoons with weapons of bladder or cow-tail to clear the way for the dancers . . . mimics or tumblers, contortionists and merry-andrews", hired professionals, whose improvised masks are often caricatures of local European officials.

It is clear, therefore, that John Canoe cannot be viewed as a single African phenomenon, transported intact to the New World. It is, rather, an intimate mixture of different West African elements, which, having undergone what the Barbadian George Lamming terms a 'sea change', emerged as a medium of creative expression for the New World African. Whatever its origin, though, one thing is sure about John

Canoe: it was this fusion of disparate elements which led all black people, wherever the festival was practised, to accept it as their own.

The John Canoe festival in the New World was predominantly a celebration which belonged to the slaves. It is perhaps this fact which led to its widespread decline after Emancipation. In Jamaica, the appearance of John Canoe and his followers grew rarer as time passed; in Belize, where the Christmas dances were performed almost exclusively by Black Caribs, John Canoe became limited to areas where they predominated; and in North Carolina, "Negro preachers," writes Ira de A. Reid, "finally succeeded in preaching the custom out of existence." Even in The Bahamas, the one place where John Canoe would not only survive into the twentieth century but grow into a living tradition, the Christmas festivities for a time assumed a particularly European air — that of a military marching band.

Why should a festival, so obviously representative of the spirit of an oppressed group, begin to die at the very moment that group was freed? Perhaps even here we may find a clue to the origin and purpose of John Canoe. Perhaps, like the tricksters who people Afro-American folklore (Ananse the spider, B'Bookie the goat, and Brer Rabbit himself) John Canoe was symbolic of the slaves' struggle to conquer their condition; evidence of their rebellion, however secret, against slavery itself. As slaves, nothing was theirs; nothing, that is, save their very 'Africanness'. As Africans, the slaves could create a complex system of self-affirmation, providing for themselves a language, a culture and an oral literature apart from those forced upon them by their masters; and the John Canoe festival was an integral part of this system. For not only did it afford the slaves a chance to express themselves in a way no European could; it also allowed them a chance to laugh. John Canoe himself, whether the representation of the chief John Conny,

Pre-Dawn Magic (Shell Bahamas Ltd)

an ancestral spirit or a *kono* dancer, was a symbol of the slaves' shared roots. His followers, by their antics and through the very characters they assumed — Captain, Lieutenant, Chief and the rest — were able to satirise the slaves' condition and ridicule the Europeans in a way no slave ordinarily could. In this light, then, John Canoe was a vehicle of survival, a tradition which gave back to the slaves for a short while the very identity slavery had removed; and Emanicipation, by freeing the Africans, took away their need for John Canoe.

There may, of course, be a very straightforward reason for the decline of John Canoe after Emancipation, one which had more to do with economics and social pressures than with the symbolic significance of the parade. The life of a slave, despite its hardships, was in certain ways less complicated than that of a freeman. For one thing, each slave was assured of the necessities of life — food, clothing, housing and the like — for as long as he or she was productive; after Emancipation, nothing of the sort was guaranteed. Secondly, the slave's year followed a rigid pattern, revolving around the state of the crop, with a holiday at Christmas, and the John Canoe festivities provided a means of celebrating that tiny bit of freedom; but Christmas, for the freeman, represented something more to work for. And thirdly, the John Canoe festivites were as much a part of the planters' Christmas as they were of their slaves'. It is no accident that throughout the New World Christmas was observed in grand style by masters and slaves alike. Not only was it a day's entertainment for them both; for the planters it was also a means of keeping order on their land. Grand Christmas celebrations were not limited to those areas which celebrated John Canoe, and for good reason; as one overseer in the Southern USA noted, after killing twenty-eight steer at Christmas for his slaves: "I can do more with [the slaves] in this way than if all the hides of the cattle were made into lashes." (Eugene D. Genovese, *Roll, Jordan, Roll: The World the Slaves Made*, New York, 1976). It is no surprise, therefore, that the masters subsidised the John Canoe festival heavily. The parades grew into expensive, time-consuming affairs as a result; and the freemen could afford neither the time nor the money to mount them. Consequently, the custom was abandoned.

Ironically, too, the African nature of the festival also worked against it. For the slaves, John Canoe had provided proof that they had identities, despite their condition, and this affirmation of their heritage was a welcome one. As freemen, however, adrift in an alien and often hostile culture, that African identity was more of a liability than a help. In North Carolina in particular, where Emancipation had not only stripped the Confederates of their economic power but was also the baggage which accompanied their defeat by the Union, it could be positively dangerous to call attention to one's blackness. It is not surprising, therefore, that John Kuner no longer exists there. Both blacks and whites opposed the festival. Religious leaders denounced it as sinful and uncivilised; "the middle class coloured," writes Reid, "looked upon the exhibition as one which lowered their status in the eyes of the whites (and) various mayors were unfavourably disposed to the practice". By 1900, the North Carolinian parade was a thing of the past.

The Bahamas remains unique in being the only country where John Canoe has neither disappeared entirely nor sunk into relative obscurity. On the contrary, the Bahamian festival has developed into an annual event of national significance. John Canoe in The Bahamas has rallied and grown, and in so doing it has outgrown itself. For it is no longer the generic New World John Canoe; it has become something unique to Bahamians. It has become the Festival of Junkanoo.

2
'Great Activity and Strength of Body'
The John Canoe Festival in the New World

Christmas, the most auspicious date in the Christian calendar of Holy Days, is observed in communities throughout the world in many different ways. Whatever the celebrations, whether religious or secular, the season generally occasions a spirit of generosity. During periods of peace, this is the time when gifts are given; during wartime, this is the interval when truces are called. It is not surprising, therefore, that it was also the period which the early English planters set aside as a holiday for their slaves.

These Africans, knowing little, if anything, about Christianity, seized the opportunity to celebrate their brief period of freedom in a way most familiar to them — by singing and dancing. From these annual slave celebrations grew a festival which spread throughout the New World. It was called the Festival of John Canoe.

Of all the British possessions in the Americas, a few stand out as homes of the festival. Among them: Jamaica, Belize, St Vincent, North Carolina, Bermuda and The Bahamas. Although little is known of the slaves' recreational activities in the New World, it is nevertheless possible to piece together a rough picture of John Canoe, using reports from travel documents, memoirs and diaries. It is possible, too, by using these descriptions, to find links between the various individual celebrations: for instance the festivals of North Carolina, The Bahamas and Bermuda have similarities, as do those of St Vincent and Belize.

As already mentioned, John Canoe was practised primarily by the slaves, and consequently declined steadily after their Emancipation in 1838. Today, John Canoe is observed only in The Bahamas on any grand scale; in the other territories, it has either disappeared completely, or is practised by a minority of inhabitants, a dying tradition. Yet once, it was among the most important slave celebrations in the English-speaking New World.

Jamaica

It was in Jamaica that the first records of the slaves' Christmas festivities were made. The earliest mention of them occurred in the seventeenth century. Sir Hans Sloane, a visitor to Jamaica in 1687, provides a valuable account of the parade:

They have likewise in their dances Rattles ty'd to their legs and wrists and in their hands with which they make a noise, keeping time with one who makes a sound answering it on the mouth of an empty Gourd or Jar with his Hand. Their dances consist of great activity and strength of Body and

Cosmic Dancers (detail from larger painting, now destroyed)

keeping time, if it can be. They very often tie Cows' Tails to their Rumps and add such others to their bodies in several places as gives them a very extraordinary appearance.

(From *A Voyage to the Islands of Madera, Barbados, Nives, St Christopher and Jamaica*, 1707.)

These dances were, no doubt, the early precursors of John Canoe dances, for the animal symbolism noted by Sloane occurs repeatedly in later accounts of the festival. The earliest specific mention of John Canoe is found in Edward Long's *History of Jamaica*, published in 1774. There, the dancers are:

several tall robust fellows dressed up in grotesque habits, and a pair of ox-horns on their heads, sprouting from the top of a horrid sort of vizor, or mask, which about the mouth is rendered very terrific with large boar-tusks. The masquerader, carrying a wooden sword in his hand, is followed with a numerous crowd of drunken women, who refresh him frequently with a cup of aniseed-water, whilst he dances at every door, bellowing out 'John Connu!' with great vehemence.

This very African John Connu quickly succumbed to the stronger culture around it, and as time passed, the celebration began to take on a more European air. By 1815, the Jamaican John Canoe dancers had begun to resemble professional English buffoons. Indeed, M.G. Lewis, a landowner in Jamaica, wrote that year of:

a Merry-Andrew dressed in a striped doublet, and bearing upon his head, a kind of pasteboard house-boat, filled with puppets, representing, some sailors, others soldiers, others again slaves at work on a plantation.

(From *Journal of a West Indian Proprietor, 1815-17*, 1929.)

Along with this radically changed John Canoe, the Set Girls became an integral part of the Christmas festivities in Jamaica. These young ladies of mixed blood were divided into two categories, the Reds and the Blues, who vied with each other in beauty and elegance of costume. After a procession through the streets, each Set led by a King and Queen, a play would be enacted before the Master at the Great House (the main residence on the plantation).

Again, the journal of M.G. Lewis proves useful. In it, he provides some explanation for the inclusion of these Set Girls in the parades. "It seems that," he writes,

> many years ago, an Admiral of the Red was superseded on the Jamaica station by an Admiral of the Blue; and both of them gave balls at Kingston to the 'Brown Girls'; for the fair sex else-where are called 'Brown Girls' in Jamaica. In consequence of these balls, all Kingston was divided into parties; from thence the division spread into other districts; and ever since, the whole island, at Christmas, is separated into rival factions of the Blues and the Reds (the Red representing also the English, the Blue the Scotch), who contend for setting forth their processions with the greatest taste and magnificence. This year, several gentlemen in the neighbourhood of Black River had subscribed very largely towards the expenses of the show; and certainly it produced the gayest and most amusing scene that I ever witnessed, to which the mutual jealousy and pique of the two parties against each other contributed to no slight degree.

The John Canoe festivities in Jamaica grew in scope and elegance year by year, and the military theme noted by Lewis continued to be favoured by the dancers. By 1837, an often-reproduced lithograph by Belisario depicts a fantastically costumed John Canoe figure in white mask, long flowing wig and regimental jacket. He wears long striped pants fitted at the ankles and festooned with bows along the sides. A broad sash encircles his waist and is tied at the back with the loose ends flowing. This figure also carries an elaborate replica of a four-storied house upon his head.

This was as far as the Jamaican John Canoe was to go. After Emancipation, first declared in 1834 but not attained fully by the slaves until 1838, the elaborate costumes and balls gradually disappeared. The play element of the tradition, however, survived well into the present century. As late as 1954 the *Caribbean Commission* carried an article by Calvin Bowen about the festival which included this description of the play:

> Only men, as a rule, take part in this annual Christmas perform-ance which has its regular 'cast' and goes through all the theatrical ritual of rehearsal . . . The music is elemental. It consists of two or three highly-pitched kettle drums (played with the fingers) . . . and one or two bamboo flutes or fifes played on the top notes only, to produce a thin reed of sound . . . Of the principal characters, apart from John Canoe himself, there is *Horsehead*, so called because he wears a giant effigy of a horse's head, covering the rest of his body with a sheet. Dressed in this weird costume, he dances and prances like a circus figure, snapping his great jaws to the twin delight and terror of children. *Cowhead*, similarly, wears a cow's head, complete with horns, and hides his body with a sheet. *Devil*, the incarnation of Old Nick himself, decks out himself in old black rags, lamp-blacks his face to show startling white teeth and red-rimmed eyes. Wearing the satanic horns and carrying the three-pronged fork, he is a creature of menace indeed. *Actor-boy*, as his name implies, is the grand mummer or 'principal boy' of this primitive Jamaican pantomime. He wears the most elaborate costume, bedecked with frills and finery; and as he whirls and pirouettes to the music of the pipes, he cuts as dashing a figure as any ballet master. *Captain*, the band leader, effects the garb and manner of a policeman . . . and

uses a whistle to start and stop the dancing sessions. He is in charge of the band. *Lieutenant*, of course assists him.

(From ''Jamaica's John Canoe'', in *Caribbean Commission*, vols 8 – 9, 1954 – 56.)

Belize and St Vincent

In Belize, where John Canoe still occurs in parts, performances may take place on Christmas Day, Boxing Day (the day after Christmas), or New Year's Day. The John Canoe dancers are masked, as they are elsewhere, and they wear elaborate head-dresses known as *wababa*, which are constructed from a cardboard frame covered with crepe paper streamers, ribbons, plumes, and glittering bits of mirror and coloured glass. The dancers, who are all male, may wear either dresses or jackets and trousers; all costumes are decorated with ribbons, sashes and streamers. None of these costumes, whether male or female, falls below the knee, so that the leg-bands worn by each dancer may be exposed. These leg-bands, or *yawai*, are strips of cloth to which hundreds of tiny shells have been sewn, and they may be heard distinctly, forming part of the accompaniment to the dance. Stockings, canvas shoes and white gloves ensure that the body is totally covered, and some of the John Canoe dancers carry a wooden sword to complete the costume.

The accompanying music, supplied by two drummers, has been compared to the military theme common to the earlier Jamaican performances. The John Canoe itself was described by Thomas Young, a visitor to St Vincent in 1847, as follows:

Heating the drum (private collection)

Soon after the music strikes up, a dancer appears, who after throwing his body into all conceivable postures, now jumping up and down grotesquely, then advancing and retreating affectedly, then after bending himself on one side so as nearly to fall down, he kicks about with great energy, till at length he gives a whirl, a bow, and retires, another taking his place until they are all exhausted.

(From *Narrative of a Residence on the Mosquito Shore*, 1847.)

It is interesting to note that the John Canoe dancers of Belize are all the descendants of the Black Caribs who were deported from St Vincent in 1797. Originally the inhabitants of Bequia, an island off the coast of St Vincent, they are the result of inter-marriage between the Caribs native to the island and uprooted West Africans. It is important to note that few of these Africans were actually slaves; the first blacks to land on Bequia were the survivors of a slave ship wrecked off its coast in 1695. These Africans, according to the nineteenth-century historian Bryan Edwards, ''were originally a race of *Mocoes*, a tribe or nation from the Bight of Benin'' (*History of the British Colonies in the West Indies*, 1807.); and they, together with the warrior Caribs, combined to form a Maroon community on Bequia. Their population was further augmented by runaway slaves from neighbouring islands.

These Black Caribs, as they came to be called, claimed Bequia for themselves, and for more than half a century maintained their sovereignty. They refused to swear allegiance to any European power, and repelled repeated attacks by British forces until finally, in 1797, they were defeated. They were then removed to Central America ''in the interest,'' wrote Sir Alan Burns one hundred and fifty years later, ''of security.'' (*History of the British West Indies*, 1965.)

The fact that the Black Caribs came originally from St Vincent, coupled with the knowledge that the cultural development of the early Vincentian slaves was relatively unrestricted, has led many researchers to seek the origin of John Canoe on that island. There is no evidence, however, that the name 'John Canoe', or any similar name, was ever used in St Vincent, despite the fact that the Christmas celebrations there closely paralleled John Canoe elsewhere in the English-speaking New World. A *Moco Jumbo* figure was, rather, the prominent feature of the Christmas festivities. In his *Narrative of a Residence on the Mosquito Shore*, Thomas Young described the 'Christmas gambols' of 1791 thus:

> Returning to the villa, we were greeted by a party which frightened the boys. It was the *Moco Jumbo* and his suite. The *Jumbo* was on stilts, with a head, mounted on the actor's head, which was concealed: the music was from two baskets, like strawberry baskets, with little bells within, shook in time. The swordsman danced with an air of menace, the musician was comical, and Jumbo assumed the 'antic terrible', and was very active on his stilts.

The stilt dancer mentioned by Young was also a common feature of the Christmas festivities in Jamaica, Belize, and The Bahamas, and residents of Bermuda in 1956 could still remember "Gombeys who first danced on stilts with, incredible as it may sound, their feet secured by thongs, but with no underbracing!" (*Dance Magazine*, May 1956.)

North Carolina

John Canoe was not, in its early days, restricted to the West Indian islands alone. In eastern North Carolina, the festival was known by various names: *John Kuner, John Kooner, John Canoe, Who-Who's,* and *joncooner*. It was celebrated at Christmas time in Wilmington, Edenton, New Bern, Windsor, Fayetteville, Southport and Hillsborough, and it resembled other parades in the British West Indies in several respects. The physician Edmund Warren, author of *A Doctor's Experience in Three Continents* (1885), provided the following description of the slaves' 'John Koonering' in Edenton in 1855:

> The leading character is the 'ragman', whose 'get-up' consists in a costume of rags, so arranged that one end of each hangs loose and dangles; two great ox horns attached to the skin of a raccoon, which is drawn over the head and face, leaving apertures only for the eyes and mouth; sandals of the skin of some wild 'varmint'; several cow or sheep bells or strings of dried goats' horns hanging about his shoulders, and so arranged as to jingle at every movement; and a short stick of seasoned wood carried in his hands.
> . . . The *second* part is taken by the best looking darkey of the place, who wears no disguise, but is simply arrayed in what they call his 'Sunday-go-to-meeting suit', and carries in his hand a small bowl or tin cup, while the other parts are arrayed fantastically in ribbons, rags, and feathers, and bearing between them several so-called musical instruments or 'gumba boxes', which consist of wooden frames covered over with tanned sheep-skins.
> . . . Coming up to the front door of the 'great house', the musicians commenced to beat their gumba-boxes violently, while characters No. 1 and No. 2 entered upon a dance of the most extraordinary character — a combination of bodily contortions, flings, kicks, gyrations and antics of every imaginable description, seemingly acting as partners, and yet each trying to excel the other in the variety and grotesqueness of his movements.

This Carolinian celebration may be compared to accounts of the early twentieth-century Junkanoo parades in The

Faces of Junkanoo (private collection)

Bahamas. As Robert Curry, author of *Bahamian Lore* (1930) observed in 1928:

> Bay Street has a carnival aspect on two occasions. From midnight to sunrise of Christmas and New Year mornings the thoroughfare is crowded densely with coloured folk wearing the most peculiar costumes. They are taking part in a ritual, the origins of which are not clear . . . Those taking part in the ceremonies are known correctly as Johnny Canoes and colloquially as Junkanoos. For weeks beforehand their costumes are being prepared. Some are exceedingly clever, being made of coloured paper cut into shreds, so that there is a swishing sound as the men walk. With such costumes the headgear is a structure, often the shape of a ship, and covered also with these shredded papers. Other costumes might represent animals, in which cases horns would often project from the covering for the heads. Everyone is masked. All carry horns and many cowbells . . . As in some of the dances of the coloured Bahamians and in some of their superstitions and pagan worship — which in solitary cases persist — so in this thoughtless jostling and hurling up and down Bay Street, back and forth, are vestiges of African rituals.

Bermuda

The gumba-boxes which provided the rhythm for the North Carolinian slaves bear many likenesses to the goombay drums which are used in Bahamian Junkanoo. In the Bermudian version of John Canoe there are dancers called *Gombeys*, and they appear on the day after Christmas to perform for the public. As late as 1956 the Gombeys were a common feature of Bermuda's Christmas celebrations; that year, in fact, *Dance Magazine* carried an article which described their actions in detail. The following account is taken from that article.

> The excitement of the crowd intensified as a tall, masked, gorgeously costumed Gombey, his four-foot head-dress of peacock feathers transforming him into a veritable giant, led his whirling dancers into a circle as he lashed the air with an enormous whip . . .

This leader, or Captain as he is called, wore a long flowing black cape bedecked with the gayest of fluttering ribbons and glittering with numerous small pieces of mirror. The warriors, with the exception of the Chief, whose cloak was shorter, were arrayed as suited their fancy and carried either hatchets or bows and arrows. Each dancer wore a grotesque mask attached to the magnificent peacock-feather headdress, colorful fringed trousers and a brief skirt covered by a small beribboned apron.

A kettle drum, two snare drums and a fife provided the musical accompaniment. The simple 2/4 marching cadence known as the 'Road Beat' gradually increased in intensity. The steady boom-boom of the big drum, the rhythms of the snares, peppered with outbursts of rimshots, electrified the audience and dancers. Both musician and performer soon departed from simplicity of beat and movement as the tempo increased. The drumming became still louder and the complex syncopated rhythms accompanied dexterous and intricate foot movements, while the torso swung violently from side to side. The Chief blew a shrill whistle. The circle of dancers continued their stampings. The Captain moved into the centre, engaging each in turn. It was obvious that a dance play was being enacted. The gyrations of the dancers became fantastic as each endeavoured to excel. The jungle-like drumming rose to fever pitch. Jumps developed into amazing leaps as, with a wild shout, the descending Gombeys executed knee slides reminescent of the finest performance of a Gene Kelly!

The rhythms segued abruptly into the Road Beat again as the dancers, now in line, acknowledged with elaborate bowings the showers of coins and applause of the spectators. The giant leader, remembering the tradition of his people, that the Gombey must perform tirelessly from sun-up to moon-set, cracked his whip! To the insistent beat of the drums, the colorful procession danced away to perform for the others.

(From Lythe Orme De Jon, ''The Gombeys of Bermuda'', in *Dance Magazine*, No. 5, May 1956.)

These scattered reports, spanning a period of some 300 years, illustrate that John Canoe flourished as the slaves' Christmas festival throughout the English-speaking New World and in some cases, it survived well into the present century. Yet it was, in the beginning, a slave tradition, one which recalled Africa for the slaves, and which celebrated that African identity which only they shared. What European characteristics it assumed were only embellishments; otherwise it remained, until the middle of the 1900s, what Robert Curry called ''a vestige of African rituals''.

3
'The Darkies are Fond of Processions'
Junkanoo in The Bahamas: The Nineteenth Century

Slavery 1800 – 1837

Little is known, anywhere in the New World, about the social activities of the Afro-American slaves in the nineteenth century. The Bahamas is no exception. Were it not for scattered reports carried in newspapers and the diary of a single estate-owner, there would be very little information indeed. Thanks to the research of Ira de A. Reid, however, we do know that a John Canoe 'king' was a 'fixture' in The Bahamas as early as 1801; and entries in the journal of Charles Farquharson, a plantation owner on San Salvador, confirm that the traditional three-day Christmas holiday was granted to Bahamian slaves. Farquharson provides what seems to be the only information relating to the slaves' observation of the holiday in his entry for Boxing Day, 1832:

Wednesday. 26. Some of our people gon [sic] abroad to see some of their friends and some at home amusing themselves in their own way threw [sic] the day, but all of them at home in the evening and had a grand dance and keep it up until near daylight.

(From *A Relic of Slavery*, Farquharson's *Journal for 1831 – 2*)

Certain factors about nineteenth century society make speculation on the Bahamian John Canoe festivities harder still.

In 1800, the Bahamian population consisted of not two, but three main groups of people: the slaves, the Loyalist settlers, and the early inhabitants of the islands. These last were proud, hardy individuals who relied upon the sea for survival. They took from it what they could, and they were, at various periods, fishermen, traders of wood and salt, wreckers and (in wartime) privateers. Theirs was a simple existence, relatively untouched by the turbulence of the age. The Loyalists, on the other hand, were the victims of that turbulence, refugees from the American War of Independence. They were a mixed lot themselves: some of them, farmers from the South, harboured hopes of becoming rich from cotton, and they settled the uninhabited islands, creating plantations whose crops flourished and failed. Others, educated men from cities like Charleston, settled in the capital and proceeded to reorganise it, building roads, schools and churches, publishing the first Bahamian newspaper, and attempting to take control of the governing of the colony.

It is small wonder that tensions in the early years ran high between the two groups. To the Bahamians, the immigrants were interfering upstarts whose activities threatened their whole way of life; the Loyalists, on the other hand, regarded the Old Inhabitants as ''[a] lower order of whites . . . a rather lawless race, the descendants of Pirates, [who] have not departed from the principles of their ancestors.'' (John Forbes,

Study of Scrap Drummer (Shell Bahamas Ltd)

Loyalist and Acting Governor of the colony, 1796.)

Even the slaves did not form a heterogeneous body. Those who had been brought to the colony by the Loyalists were, for the most part, field labourers who were taken to the Out Islands to work on plantations. Those who belonged to the early Bahamian settlers were, like their masters, urban and seafaring people, employed as managers, artisans and boatmen. Unlike their counterparts in the rest of the West Indies, the Bahamian slaves did not even have the fortune of mingling with one another; for the whole of the Bahamian population was scattered among some nine or more islands, each of them isolated from the other and from the capital.

As a result, no practice recorded in any single part of the archipelago can be presumed common to the whole colony. The 'grand dance' noted by Farquharson in San Salvador was the way Christmas was celebrated on that island. As we shall see, it was observed rather differently in the capital, and each of the other islands, no doubt, had a tradition of its own.

Two conclusions, however, may be drawn about the Bahamian Christmas festivities before Emancipation. One is that such activities did exist, and that they involved the slaves. The other is that, wherever these activities were found, they seemed to bear resemblance to the John Canoe celebrations held elsewhere in the Americas.

Post-Emancipation 1838 – 1865

It has already been noted that John Canoe, primarily a festival belonging to the slaves, underwent a transformation during the years following Emancipation. The Bahamas does not seem to have been excluded from this trend. One other thing which may be safely assumed about the early Bahamian versions of John Canoe parades is that, whatever their form, they had a distinctly African flavour. The celebrations in Nassau in the 1840s show a marked change. It was the custom then for the Royal Militia Band to bring in Christmas morning with music; the Market on Bay Street was the hub of activity, and was open from the early hours of the morning until 9 a.m. It was here that John Canoe and his followers danced — to what music we do not know — on stilts.

Another Christmas Day has passed, and the festivities of old have commenced 'right merrily'. The Yule Log and Wassail Cup of our fatherland are not seen here, — but these are not the only signs of Christmas. We have in this distant isle other, and as cheering reminiscences of the period, and, although no carrol [sic] is sung, the morn is ushered in with music. The Militia Band and the fifes and drums of the Regiment break on the slumber'd ear, and answer for the 'Waites'; and the sound of footsteps at the dawn of the day, added to the din of voices and the noise of 'crackers', give intimation of the joyous season.

The markets were open yesterday until 9 a.m. They were unusually thronged, and the show of meat and vegetables was extremely good. Several prize oxen, decked out in ribbons, were led over the town, previous to falling a sacrifice, and 'John Canoe' came forth on stilts in style, much to the gratification of his numerous train of followers. Christmas has commenced well, and we trust it will end so. We wish our friends and patrons the usual compliments of the season.

(From *The Nassau Guardian*, December 26, 1849.)

As well as the stilt dancers, which remained a part of the festival until the 1940s, two other characters, *Neptune* and *Amphitrite*, also made an appearance each year. The first mention of these characters is found in the *Guardian* of December 30th, 1854.

Christmas with its customary festivities has been passed by all classes of the inhabitants of our little isle, amidst much mirth and gladness. Christmas Day was ushered in by the sound of music from the Militia Band and closed by the burning of an effigy of the *soi-disant* 'Peripatetic', which last contributed not a little towards the amusement of those who live in the Eastern district where it was burnt. Various grotesque figures, intended to represent Neptune, Amphitrite and others preceded by fifes and tambourines have on succeeding days exhibited themselves in our usually quiet streets exciting the greatest merriment among the lower orders.

It perhaps seems strange that these two characters from Greek and Roman mythology should find themselves in the midst of what was essentially a West African festival in The Bahamas. The answer, however, may lie in the sea-faring nature of the Bahamian people. Neptune, states the *Dictionary of Mythology, Folklore and Symbols* (1961), is an "ancient Italian divinity of moisture, provider of the perpetuity of springs and streams . . . identical with Poseidon as chief god of the sea." He is "portrayed as a stately elderly bearded man carrying a trident, sometimes astride a dolphin or horse." Amphitrite, according to the same source, is, in Greek mythology, the wife of Poseidon and Queen of the moaning sea. It is she who sends out sea-monsters, she who drives waves against the rocks; and she is depicted as a Nereid (sea-nymph) of queenly mien, her moist flowing hair bound in a net.

The character of Neptune was central to traditional initiation practices performed at sea. Horace Beck, in his work *Folklore and the Sea* (1973), notes that certain rites were carried out on a new sailor which, once endured, "welcomed him into the ranks of . . . seasoned sailors." When one crossed 180° longitude, for instance, one became a Member of the Order of the Golden Dragon; upon crossing the Equator, one was made 'a son of Neptune'. The initiation rites used stemmed from the ancient seaman's belief that tidal currents and disturbed waters were the work of submarine monsters and that, in order to appease these, some sort of ritual — which varied from prayer to human sacrifice — had to be performed. As human knowledge of the sea became more sophisticated, the sacrifice of human victims to the sea-gods was abandoned, and by the end of the sixteenth century, the ceremonies had acquired their modern forms.

Characteristic of the ritual of crossing the Equator was a visit from Neptune — or, to be realistic, someone disguised as Neptune. Sometimes he was alone; sometimes, however, he was accompanied by his wife Amphitrite, and a motley court. Any young sailor 'crossing the line' for the first time was seized by Neptune, who, with the help of the crew, lathered the poor novice's face with tar, shaved him roughly, and then doused him with salt water. If the green hand survived this ordeal, he was then proclaimed a 'son of Neptune'.

Although Beck's book makes no mention of the fact, these initiation ceremonies also occurred at the crossing of the Tropic of Cancer. In her journal, Lady Nugent, wife of Sir Charles Nugent, Governor of Jamaica, describes her first crossing into the tropics, and the activities of the crew are very similar to those which occur at the crossing of the Equator:

> 29th [June 1801] — Pass the Tropic. Neptune and Amphitrite came on board, and there was a masquerade throughout the whole day. General N. and I were unmolested, and allowed to see all the sport without any annoyance. Some poor men were sadly pulled about, and shaved in the roughest manner, though all was done in perfect good humour.

(From Frank Cundall (ed.), *Lady Nugent's Journal: Jamaica One Hundred Years Ago*, 1907.)

Rhythmic Drummer (Shell Bahamas Ltd)

There are no available descriptions of the costumes worn by the Bahamian Neptune and Amphitrite. In order to be recognised as such, however, they must have been dressed in costumes closely resembling those worn at sea. Of interest, therefore, is the following description of Neptune's appearance as seen on a sea voyage in the 1870s:

A navy blue blanket for a robe, thrown over his head and fastened under the chin, was draped over his shoulders and trailed behind. Its edges were trimmed with gulf-weed, and bunches of rope-yarn, painted green to give it the effect of the sea, were sewn on for the occasion. He wore a crown which had two holes cut for the eyes, and another for the nose, which protruded and was also painted red, while around his mouth and over his chin was a fringe of rope-yarn, for whiskers, the ends of which were picked out, blossoming into bunches of oakum over which he frequently squirted tobacco juice. In his right hand he carried a five-pronged grains-iron fitted with a pole, for a trident, from which dangled pieces of rope-yarn to give the effect of green seaweed and in his left hand was a speaking trumpet. His big sea boots were much too large, but were in keeping with the rest of his costume.

(From Frederick Pease Harlow, *The Making of a Sailor*, 1928.)

It must be noted that the sea-rituals associated with Neptune appear to have certain elements in common with the Bahamian John Canoe. To begin with, as Lady Nugent noted in her journal, costumes and masks were part of the ceremonies. What is more, the figures of Neptune and his wife were fantastic enough to capture the imagination of any 'Johnny Canoe'. Small wonder, then, that they were incorporated into the Bahamian parades.

We have every reason to believe that the sea god and goddess first appeared not in Nassau, but in one of the southeastern islands of the chain, possibly Inagua. To begin with, these are the only Bahamian islands lying south of the Tropic of Cancer. Moreover the mid 1800s were the most prosperous years those islands had ever seen. In 1849, the Heneaga Salt Pond Company was established to develop the Inagua salt flats. As a result, Inagua, the third largest Bahamian island and rich in salt, experienced a boom which sustained it well into the early decades of the twentieth century; and for the next twenty-five years, Matthew Town, Inagua, was one of the busiest ports in the archipelago. At its peak, Inagua exported one-and-a-half million bushels of salt a year and there was heavy sea traffic between that island and the north. If, indeed, the initiation ceremonies took place on every ship crossing the Tropic of Cancer on its way to Inagua, then the figures of Neptune and Amphitrite would have been very familiar to every Inaguan sailor.

Another reason for placing the origin of Neptune and Amphitrite in Inagua is that island's proximity to Haiti. The impact of Haitian culture upon The Bahamas, particularly upon the southeastern islands of the archipelago, is a subject which has yet fully to be explored. The fact that Inagua lies not sixty miles off the north coast of Hispaniola suggests that this island ought to have some cultural ties with Haiti. A quick survey of surnames from Inagua and the neighbouring islands indicates that such ties may exist: names like Bonamy, Godet, Duvalier and Symonette all point to a French or Créole root. It was not uncommon for wealthy Inaguans of the nineteenth century to travel to Port-au-Prince rather than to Nassau in order to shop or visit the doctor, just as today inhabitants of Grand Bahama and Bimini frequent Miami. Some Inaguan children were even educated in Haiti where the French heritage was considered more refined than anything Nassau might have to offer. Similarities between Bahamian and Haitian folklore indicate that ties may exist with the more northerly Bahamas as well. The familiar characters of B'Bookie and

B'Rabbie, the simple-minded goat and his trickster friend, for example, are almost identical to the Haitian Compère Bouki and Compère Lapin.

It should come as no surprise, then, that included in the pantheon of Haitian divinities are the figures of Agwé, Lord of the Sea, and his consort, La Sirène. In the Voudou calendar, the days set aside for the festival of Agwé — the 'Feeding of the Sea' — are December 12th, 13th and 14th; and in the Bahamian calendar, the traditional Junkanoo season ran from Guy Fawkes' Night (November 5th) until New Year's Day. Of Agwé, the anthropologist Alfred Métraux writes:

> The sea with all its flora and fauna, as well as the ships which plough its surface and those who live off its produce, all come under his jurisdiction . . . his emblems are miniature boats, oars painted blue and green, shells . . . and sometimes small metal fishes . . . This Haitian Neptune also has a trident as part of his insignia . . . Like many aquatic spirits, [his] symbolic colour is white [and] he is depicted as a mulatto with a fair skin and eyes as green as the sea. He wears the uniform of a naval officer, white gloves and a helmet.
>
> (From *Voodoo in Haiti*, 1959.)

It is interesting to note that figures of boats and the like were common in Junkanoo even as late as the 1950s. Of course, in a society which relies so heavily on the sea for its income, this is not surprising, but it is also very likely that the Haitian Agwé had some influence on the development of Junkanoo.

The south-eastern Bahamas, then, must be regarded as central to the appearance of Neptune and Amphitrite in Bahamian Junkanoo. That the figures first appeared in Inagua is borne out by the statements of several older Inaguans interviewed in 1977. These people remembered that in their

Rhythmic Cow Bells (Shell Bahamas Ltd)

Junkanoo parades, an *Old Neptune* figure took part in the celebrations. In addition, an informant in nearby Ragged Island mentioned that, although Junkanoo was unknown there, Neptune did appear at Christmas. Usually accompanied by two or three followers, this character went from door to door in the community, singing and dancing for the public.

While Neptune continued to roam the streets of Inagua and Ragged Island every Christmas, both he and his Queen soon disappeared in Nassau. By 1857, we read of their demise in the December 30th edition of the *Nassau Guardian*:

> If we except the noise made by Chinese crackers and other fireworks, the festivities of Christmas have passed off quietly enough in our little isle. The representatives of the illustrious 'Johnny Canoe' of former days have dwindled down to two or three, and as for 'Neptune and Amphitrite' they have not left their watery domain at all this season.

By the late 1850s it would appear that John Canoe in The Bahamas, as elsewhere, was fast approaching extinction. The Bahamian festival, however, was not yet a thing of the past; and certain factors were present in Bahamian society which prevented it from dying out completely.

The first was the relative unimportance, for white Bahamians, of the custom during slavery. Never a sugar-producer, the colony early developed a diversified economy, and the resulting society was never tightly anchored to the plantation. Plantations there were in The Bahamas; but these were relatively recent introductions, created by the Loyalists during the last quarter of the eighteenth century to grow cotton. The majority of these plantations were spread among the 'agricultural' islands of the south and central Bahamas, where populations were small. The decline of the cotton industry at the turn of the nineteenth century led to the diversification of crops and skills, thus creating communities whose members quickly learned the virtues of self-reliance.

In the northern Bahamas, which had had a longer period of settlement, the populations continued their traditional ways of life — fishing, subsistence farming, wrecking and trading. Again, in contrast to Jamaica, most slave holdings were small; as a result, masters and slaves alike developed attitudes of individualism which discouraged the growth of such community-based traditions as John Canoe.

In the capital, whose economy depended more on trade and business than on agriculture, society was still more diverse and slaves were employed in all manner of jobs. The community which grew up as a result was fragmented, and it is quite likely that the recreational activities of the slaves were of little interest to the whites. In 1834, notes Dr Gail Saunders,

> New Providence contained Nassau, the capital and chief port. It had a growing seafaring population and also more diversified occupations in the various trades such as butchers, bakers and masons . . . By 1834, four slaves were employed in Government departments, two were warehousemen [and] one was a watchman. [Domestics made up] the dominant occupational group in New Providence.

> (From *Slavery in The Bahamas, 1648 – 1838*, 1985.)

As a result, the lives of the masters, unlike those of their Jamaican counterparts, were often kept separate from those of their slaves. The Bahamian John Canoe, while possibly a source of entertainment for the whites, would not have been as much a part of the masters' holidays as it was elsewhere in the West Indies. What was more, the white Bahamians, few of them wealthy landowners, would have been unable — and probably unwilling — to lend their support to the parade in

Goodmans Bay Goombay (private collection in USA)

any material way.

The result of this was twofold. The Bahamian festival of the early nineteenth century was never the elaborate show that John Canoe was in Jamaica; it was a festival celebrated almost exclusively by the slaves. This meant, ironically, that the Bahamian John Canoe (or Junkanoo), never dependent upon the whites for survival, was not affected economically by Emancipation; the festival was still the property of the blacks, and consequently continued to be held long years after that date.

The celebration of Guy Fawkes' Day, a custom peculiar to the British, was a second factor which contributed to the preservation of the festival. Guy Fawkes was one of a band of English Catholics who, dissatisfied with the policies of James I towards their religion, plotted his assassination. This was to be achieved by blowing up the Houses of Parliament while the King was in them, and the date was set for early November, 1605. The unfortunate Fawkes, however, left to guard the gunpowder, was captured, and the plot revealed. He was later executed for high treason.

In remembrance of this ill-fated 'Gunpowder Plot', the night of November 5th, named after Fawkes, is one of celebration in Britain. Fireworks are let off, a bonfire built, and, at the peak of the evening, an effigy of Guy Fawkes burnt. This custom, patriotic in the extreme, was transported by the English to their colonies, where it was adopted whole-heartedly. In The Bahamas, new elements were incorporated into the celebrations: cowbells, whistles, horns and drums, the music of Junkanoo. To many a Bahamian, Guy Fawkes' Day represented the beginning of another Junkanoo season; and instruments taken out for the Fifth of November were often not put away until after the New Year. Often, long after the Guy Fawkes celebrations were over, one could still hear little groups of musicians practising for Christmas.

Strange as it may at first seem, Guy Fawkes' Night shared several elements with mid-nineteenth-century Junkanoo. Both fireworks and the burning of effigies have been mentioned as part of the nineteenth-century Christmas festivities in Nassau. This fact, coupled with the proximity of Guy Fawkes' Day to Christmas, leads almost naturally to an association of the two dates. Guy Fawkes' Day, for the true Junkanoo enthusiast, was as good a time as any to begin earnest rehearsal for the Christmas parade.

A third factor, and perhaps the most significant, was the landing in The Bahamas, between 1811 and 1860, of over 6,000 Liberated Africans.

In 1807, the British Government abolished the capture and sale of Africans to its New World colonies. It also decreed that any slaves taken in battle with foreign ships must be set free on British soil, and in this way declared subtle economic war on its rivals in the West Indies. British seamen immediately took it upon themselves to intercept French, Spanish, Portuguese and American ships bound for the New World, capturing them and freeing the Africans on board.

The Bahamas, conveniently situated off the coasts of both the United States and Cuba, was a fertile hunting ground for such ships. In addition, its treacherous waters made it the site of several wrecks, and many of the Africans taken from slave ships were settled in the archipelago. By the end of the 1830s, over 5,000 Liberated Africans had been landed in The Bahamas.

The arrival of the Liberated Africans had a profound effect on the growth of the [Bahamian] population. [In 1834], there were more free blacks per square mile (36.9) in New Providence than whites (17.7) or slaves (28.1).

(From Dr Gail Saunders, *Slavery in The Bahamas, 1648 – 1838*, 1985.)

Significant for the preservation and development of Junkanoo was not only the number of these Africans, but also their origins. In 1800, a substantial number of the Bahamian blacks, slave and free, had been born in the Americas. As a result, their African heritage was fragmented at best — hence the very European air of certain Christmas celebrations, such as the music played by the Royal Militia Band. The Liberated Africans, on the other hand, never slaves, and forced to settle in communities apart from those already in existence, were far more able to preserve that heritage. As well as the appearance of John Canoe on Christmas Day, 1849, there was a sacrifice of oxen — evidence of the new African presence in the community.

In a 1984 article on the settlement of African recaptives in The Bahamas, Professor Peter Dalleo writes:

in the 19th century The Bahamas received a more ethnically diversified population than has been understood. The recaptives brought to The Bahamas offer a good example of widespread geographical and cultural variation. Like most slaves carried across the Atlantic, the recaptives came as part of a mixed cargo. For example [in 1811] the *Isabella* held the following: Mocco, Papir Mongola, Camaloo, and Ebo. Five years later the *Rosa* transported Congo, Crou, Kipee, Ebo, Mocca, Mongola, and Mohambu peoples. In 1828, in addition to the already-mentioned groups, the collector of customs listed the following in his report: Benin, Bibe, Gamba, Gola, Hanga, Hausa, Mondingo, and Koromantee. Many of the ships captured in the 1830s conveyed peoples from the Congo region.

(From ''Africans in the Caribbean: A Preliminary Assessment of Recaptives in The Bahamas, 1811 – 1860'', in the *Journal of Bahamas Historical Society*, October 1984.)

The varied backgrounds of these Africans raise many questions about the development of Bahamian Junkanoo. We have already seen, for instance, how the figures of Neptune and Amphitrite may be connected to Haitian divinities. When we consider that these divinities had their roots in Benin and the Nago territories of the Yoruba people, we are immediately drawn to the idea that perhaps certain Liberated Africans, when confronted with those figures — whether Neptune on board ship, or Agwé in Haiti or Inagua — recognised them and adopted them as part of their Christmas celebrations.

Depression 1866 – 1899

The 1860s in The Bahamas were years of economic extremes. They opened with the banging guns of the American Civil War, and wealth gained from smuggling supplies into blockaded Confederate ports flooded the capital; they limped out in the trail of the Great Bahama Hurricane of 1866, which swept through the whole archipelago, leaving nothing untouched. By the end of that decade, the prosperity of the war years having disappeared as quickly as it had come, the colony was entering a period of depression which would not lift until the 1920s. It would have been understandable if, eclipsed first by the frenzy of blockade days, and then by the poverty which followed, Junkanoo in The Bahamas, as elsewhere, had declined. And as we have seen, the late 1850s do record a sharp drop in participation in the Nassau parades. It is highly likely that the descendants of the Free Africans were largely responsible for the preservation of the custom. But in the 1880s, another factor emerged which also helped keep the tradition alive — the involvement of whites.

L.D. Powles, Circuit Magistrate in The Bahamas during the 1880s, observed in 1888:

I doubt if any of them have the least notion of who Guy Fawkes was, or what he did, but they would not omit observing Guy Fawkes' Day on any consideration. Every 5th November his effigy is carried in procession with bands of music and torches, and solemnly hung on a gallows prepared for that purpose. The darkies are fond of processions, and never miss an opportunity of getting one up.

About Christmas time they seem to march about day and night with lanterns and bands of music, and they fire off crackers everywhere. This is a terrible nuisance, but the custom has the sanction of antiquity, though no doubt it would have been put down long ago if the white young gentlemen had not exhibited a taste for the same amusement.

(From *The Land of the Pink Pearl*, 1888.)

This phenomenon is unique in the history of pre-Independence Junkanoo. One explanation is that, after the 1830s, Junkanoo came to be viewed increasingly as the natural way to pass a Bahamian Christmas.

The events of subsequent decades were destabilising to the colony and to the society of the time. First, in 1851, an outbreak of cholera in the city left many dead. A decade later came the turbulent years of the American Civil War, which, though soon over, turned the community on its head. Michael Craton, describing that time, comments: "Nassau has never known a more frenzied interlude before or since." (From *A History of The Bahamas*, 1986.) Radical times often bring radical responses. Whatever the reason, young white Bahamians of the contemporary ruling merchant class participated freely in the festival during these turbulent years.

By the end of the century, however, Junkanoo was once more the property of the blacks. By that time, it had also regained its place as an established tradition; the Christmas festivities were beginning to assume certain features which would later be identified with the twentieth-century parade — features which would reinforce their significance for Bahamians.

From the end of the blockade running in 1865 until the decline of the pineapple industry in the early 1900s, Bahamians were engaged in commercial ventures of various kinds which inevitably had one end — failure. By the 1890s, therefore, employment was scarce. The colony had endured nearly thirty years of unrelieved economic depression, and everyone was poor. It is therefore no surprise that the *Nassau Guardian* of December 24th, 1890, should publish the following notice:

We have been informed that tomorrow morning a Masked Army will muster on Eastern Parade whence they will proceed down Bay Street to the Royal Victoria Hotel grounds, and then to Government Hill where they will deliver an address to His Excellency the Governor. The members of the army are young mechanics and cigar makers who are desirous of obtaining advice as to whether they shall go to Cuba or wait here for employment. They are supposed to arrive at Government Hill at six o'clock, and at eight o'clock to partake of a breakfast with a few of their invited friends.

The period of the year (Christmas), the time of day (early morning), and the masks of the marchers leave little doubt that they were Junkanoos. The tradition of marching to the Governor's residence was one not unfamiliar to Bahamians of the era. Every year on Emancipation Day, it was the custom, particularly in hard times, for representatives of various communities to parade to Government Hill and present the British Governor with petitions. These processions were often organised by the combined Friendly Societies of Nassau and here they have something in common with the parade mentioned above. A later report in the same newspaper states that the Christmas marchers were led by the Grant's Town Friendly Society Band.

What is also interesting about this parade is that the participants are once again black. Their occupations (mechanics and cigar makers) and the fact that they were led by a band from one of the black settlements attest to this; no longer are we reading of the 'white young gentlemen' who took part in earlier Junkanoo parades. The custom of whites taking part in Junkanoo was short-lived, little more than a fad.

As we have seen, the Friendly Societies responsible for the above march were essentially African in origin. Later to adopt the names and styles of various Masonic Lodges, they played a major role in the lives of black Bahamians. At the close of the nineteenth century, they not only provided their members with simple privileges they might otherwise be unable to afford — the arrangement of decent funerals, for instance — but they also oversaw various social activities, and worked to protect the interests of the communities they served.

The 1890s, then, saw the earliest documented accounts of Junkanoo being used as an agent for social change. The face of the festival itself was changing. No longer was it merely the black people's way of keeping a holiday. In it, rather, we can detect the beginnings of the social power which resides in today's Junkanoo. These late nineteenth-century parades can be seen as the forerunners of the modern practice of mobilising political support through Junkanoo.

If the face of Junkanoo was changing, it was assuming more than one aspect. In one respect, it was being used as a catalyst for positive social action. It had a second, quite different side, however, one which led to its being curtailed. Other Junkanoo parades were not nearly as orderly as the procession which made its way up Government Hill in 1890.

In his work *The Wretched of the Earth* (1963), Frantz Fanon, renowned Martinican psychologist, remarked upon the

Head-dress and shoulder-piece (private collection)

tendency of oppressed groups of people towards violence. Often, because they feel helpless to improve their condition, that violence is directed at themselves. He wrote:

> The colonised man will first manifest [the] aggressiveness which has been deposited in his bones against his own people. This is the period when [Negroes] beat each other up, and the police and magistrate do not know which way to turn when faced with . . . astonishing waves of crime.

The black Bahamians of the 1890s faced oppression on all fronts — a ruling white merchant class above them, and unbroken poverty all around. With employment scarce and money short, Christmas for them was little more than a time to express their frustration. It is no wonder, then, that the Junkanoo parades of this period began to resemble mock brawls rather than seasonal celebrations.

As the colony approached the turn of the century the Government became alarmed at the indiscriminate marching about 'day and night' at Christmas time. In 1899, a new Act, the Street Nuisances Prohibition Act, came into effect. As its name implies, its purpose was to banish 'nuisances' from the streets for most of the year. In order to allow time for legitimate parades, however, the rules of the Act were waived four times a year: from six to ten p.m. on December 24th and 31st, and from four to nine on Christmas and New Year's mornings. The Government was formalising a tradition which had until then been simply customary — the practice of holding Junkanoo parades in the early morning. Of the two periods, the participants in the parade quickly demonstrated their preference for the morning times. According to some of the older Nassauvians interviewed in 1977, only semi-costumed stragglers who wished to 'let off steam' bothered to come out in the evenings. The 'real' Junkanoo parades — complete with costumes and music — took place on Bay Street just before dawn.

4
'Bake De Johnny Cake, Chrismas Comin''
Junkanoo in The Bahamas: 1900 – 1919

It is not surprising that few specific references are made to Junkanoo in the early twentieth century. The festival was once more the exclusive property of Bahamians of African descent, and these, like the slaves a century before them, were poorly represented in the literature of the time. There is no reason to suppose, however, that Junkanoo was similarly absent from Bahamian life. On the contrary; the first decades of the twentieth century were the years when the seeds of modern Junkanoo were sown.

In the first place, the Street Nuisances Act of 1899 had had the effect of relegating the festival to specific dates and times. No longer, for instance, would it be common for Junkanoo celebrations to begin on Guy Fawkes' Day and continue unbridled until January 1st; the celebrations were now firmly anchored to their place in the Christmas season. Again, perhaps as a result of the Act, the festival began to take on a new form, one which would be familiar to the modern spectator. For the first time, the references to Junkanoo in the early 1900s mention that the masqueraders were appearing in Junkanoo bands.

These changes can be followed in the newspaper reports of the age. The 1890 procession to Government Hill, the disorderly conduct which prompted the 1899 legislation and the ''grotesque masqueraders'' of 1911 whose ''energy and vigour'' were remarked upon by the then editor of the *Tribune*

are all quite different from one another. Whereas, in 1899, the Junkanoos had abandoned orderly processions in favour of spontaneity, by 1911 they had assumed an order of a different kind. When the cultural anthropologist Amelia Defries visited Nassau in 1913, she found Junkanoo an event in which street gangs, each headed by a leader, charged or 'rushed' up and down Bay Street to the music of their drums. (A 'rush' is a Junkanoo parade without large costumes, during which participants march or dance speedily and make music.) According to informants who were young people during the early 1900s, these gangs represented the various neighbourhoods of the town. As they rushed, their leaders would dance ''backwards in a curious kind of *pas seul* — one step forward and two steps back'' (Defries, *In a Forgotten Colony*, 1917.), and in this way carry their groups the length of Bay Street. The festival had come a long way from the procession of 1890.

That Junkanoo should change so much in twenty years is not surprising, given the circumstances of the age. The first decades of the twentieth century, like the last ones of the nineteenth, were, for Bahamians, characterised by unrelieved economic depression. The last financial boom had been occasioned in the 1860s by the American Civil War, and the next would not come until Prohibition and the Roaring Twenties brought wealth. Various schemes for improving the economy had been tried and exhausted, so that by the 1900s poverty was widespread. Certain industries — sponging, tourism during the winter, and the cultivation of sisal, pineapples and tomatoes — continued to provide a number of people with jobs, but these jobs were limited, and precarious at best. For employers, high tariffs and falling prices on the world market had cut profits to a minimum, and cash was scarce. Payment of their workers, therefore, was given according to the truck system — not in cash, but in articles of clothing, rations of food and portions of the produce.

In an effort to combat the growing poverty of the age, scores of men, the majority of them from the Out Islands, looked outside the colony for jobs. These were most often to be had in Florida, Mexico or Central America, and many Bahamian men left home to work on the Panama Canal, the Mexican Central Railway, or the mahogany forests of Nicaragua and Guatemala. Work as stevedores was also available on the ships of the Hamburg-Amerika shipping line, a German company whose vessels called at Long Cay and Inagua in the southeastern Bahamas on their way to South America. As a result, many of the labourers who left home were exposed to life of a far different quality than they had known, and this fact would have unforeseen consequences later in the century.

For a short while the island of Abaco in the northern Bahamas attracted a number of workers. During the 1900s, it was the site of the Bahama Lumber Company, an American concern which had set up business at Wilson City, Abaco; and it was here that black Bahamians first experienced segregation, along American lines, on their native soil. Wilson City was remarkable in more ways than one. For a while, because of its American connection, its facilities were more modern than those of the capital; when Nassau received electricity in 1909, the labourers at Wilson City had already had theirs for a year.

The resulting population of the colony was a migrant one. Able-bodied men were commonly absent or unemployed, and

Scrap Dancer with Cowbells I (private collection)

women the heads of their households. The black labouring population was becoming more cosmopolitan in experience and thinking than the white elite; and those people who had worked for Americans had been exposed to more racial hatred than any Bahamians of an earlier age.

Nassau, consequently, was changing. The government was easing the colony into the modern age with the careful introduction of modern conveniences — the first automobile in 1905, telephones in 1907 and electric light two years later — and the town itself was assuming new, twentieth-century dimensions. Its population was growing, thanks to sizable numbers of Out Islanders who still migrated to the capital in the hope of finding jobs. For those who planned to leave the colony to find work, too, Nassau was a natural port of call; and the town's numbers were being further augmented by the arrival of foreigners, among them Greek spongers, Oriental and Semitic merchants, and assorted West Indians. Almost unnoticed by the elite, Nassau was ceasing to be the small, ordered town it had become after the Loyalist settlement. It was beginning to take on some of the attributes of an urban centre, and with these, an age of carefully-delineated social strata and unquestioned conventions was drawing to a close.

The resulting disquiet was reflected in the Junkanoo parades. The masked gangs which convened on Bay Street during the Christmas season were not there with the single purpose of celebrating the holiday; all too often their members had come out to settle old scores. As has been noted, each gang represented a different area of the town. In those days, Nassau was divided into the Western, Southern, Eastern and City Districts, each of which had its own representatives in Parliament. These divisions functioned as more than mere political boundaries; each was a community in its own right, and people from other districts were viewed with hostility.

Fringed Head-dress (private collection)

The Junkanoo parades of the time consisted of gangs from different districts marching speedily, or 'rushing', from one end of Bay Street to the other. Not surprisingly, the clashes which occurred when one group met another on its way back were apt to end in brawls. Winston Saunders' description of Junkanoo in the 1930s applies equally well to the early twentieth-century parades:

[Junkanoo] allowed for what I call tribal warfare. There was a time when people born in the east [of Nassau] could not very easily cross over Nassau Street to come into the west without explaining themselves. So there was 'gang' warfare involved in Junkanoo. So there was disguise.

(Winston Saunders, interview with Keith Wisdom, December 12th 1984, in Wisdom's *Bahamian Junkanoo: An Act in a Modern Social Drama*, PhD Dissertation, 1985.)

It is said that Nassauvians waited patiently for Christmas, when, under cover of Junkanoo costumes, they could avenge themselves on persons who had done them wrong during the year. The metal cowbells and whips carried by some stood them in good stead on these occasions.

The festive season of the pre-War era was also a period for tricks and pranks. At Christmas time, the young men of the community would remove gates and fences from their hinges, obstruct the streets with boxes and carts, and remove bridges covering water drains. Such a nuisance did they prove that the *Tribune* of December 27th, 1913, advocated that they:

should have the knowledge injected into them through the medium of their dermis with a cat-o-nine-tails and lengthened curtailment of the liberty, which they put to such ill use.

The newspapers took a dim view of Junkanoo on the whole.

For the *Nassau Guardian*, published by the white, upper-class Moseley family and read by Bahamians of the same ilk, the festival was one of those "vestiges of African ritual" noted by Robert Curry in his 1928 book, *Bahamian Lore*. As such, the parade was rarely mentioned by that journal at all. The *Tribune*, established by Leon Dupuch in 1903 with a view to giving coloured Bahamians a voice, tended to treat the festival in much the same way as middle-class blacks had the North Carolinian John Kuner some decades before. Many respectable Bahamians looked upon the rushing up and down Bay Street as a senseless waste of energy, and the *Tribune*'s editorial of January 3rd, 1911, voiced the sentiments of them all:

The New Year holiday was heralded early on Monday morning by the customary noise of horns, bells and drums and the grotesque masqueraders disported themselves along Bay Street with an energy and vigour which if put into their pursuit of their avocations during the year will be to some purpose.

All in all, this newspaper was anything but sympathetic to the junkanoos. In a nostalgic commentary on December 24th, 1913, the editor wrote:

Yes! In the old days slumbers were undisturbed in the early hours of Christmas morning . . . When we woke up in the old days it was to hear the melody of the militia band, serenading their officers and local officials, or the less pretentious fiddle and tambourine orchestra serenading their patrons or the revellers enjoying in their own way the pleasing assurance that 'Christmas comes but once a year'.

Things have changed and we are forced to admit not for the better. The dawn of the great festival is now ushered in by a senseless din of discordant horns and bells by no means silver-toned, and the beating of anything that can make a noise.

A horrible incongruous celebration of the Nativity of 'The Prince of Peace'.

The 'grotesque masqueraders' of the 1911 editorial wore costumes very different from those seen today. Money was scarce and fabric limited, and the costumes were therefore made from any cheap materials available. Newspaper, sponge, banana leaves, tissue paper and 'crocus sack' — the coarse brown sacking in which imported foods were contained — all played their part. The body was always completely covered, the face disguised, and a fantastic hat was worn on the head. The costumes which resulted were highly inventive, and often frightening as well. Hats were usually conical with broad brims, like those of picture-book witches, or they took the shape of large wasps' nests; and faces were blackened with charcoal, whitened with flour, or else concealed behind a mask.

This last — the most pervasive aspect of the festival — was the most horrifying part of a Junkanoo's attire. The mask might consist simply of a stocking drawn over the head, a cardboard construction cut out by hand, or an affair made of gauze and wire and painted for effect. The most terrifying masks, however, were the 'sifter faces': store-bought, and made from a wiry, gauze-like material. Pinkish-white in colour and totally devoid of expression, they were contoured and had two slits for the eyes. Where they originated is not known; one person interviewed in 1977 thought that they were imported from Germany, while another suggested that they might have been Japanese.

The masks might well have come from Germany. Ships of both the Hamburg-Amerika and the Royal Netherlands Lines passed regularly through the archipelago, stopping at Inagua and Long Cay, carrying Bahamian labourers south to Central America. In addition, Bahamians often took jobs as stevedores on the ships themselves. So it is not unlikely that masks made in Germany, like the Mediterranean figures of Neptune and Amphitrite some generations before, should find their way into the Junkanoo parades.

The idea that the masks could have come from Japan, while improbable, must certainly have been suggested by the slit eyes and expressionless features of the 'sifter faces', which combined to produce an oriental effect. But oriental-style masks were also worn by certain African tribes as shown in the following extract from Franco Monti's 1969 book, *African Masks*:

The Balumbo group — composed of different tribes scattered over Gabon and the republic of the Congo, such as the M'Pongwe, the Mashango, the Eshira and the Bakota — find the basic expression of their own art in the mask. The most noted and widely spread mask shows a graceful female face, which is white under the dark elaborate hair-style, with elongated eyes, and lips parted in a light enigmatic smile. There is a surprising resemblance to certain theatrical masks of the Far East. The masks are worn by the initiates of the *mukuy* society in a dance performed on stilts and are thought to have the function of symbolising the spirits of the dead.

The creative individuality of the Junkanoo costumes of the era was noted by Amelia Defries in her description of the 1916 Christmas masquerade in Nassau.

The general impression I got as daylight broke was a mass of people who had been looting one of the Natural History Museums in New York and had then gone crazy! The masks were cheap and machine made and were in imitation of white people.

When dawn broke ... the Commandant appeared, immaculate in white, and he seemed oblivious to the fact that in the dancing throng there were more than one parody of his uniform! There was even a 'kiltie', and there was a parody of a British M.A. The latter never danced at all, but walked sedately, carrying a book and umbrella — always alone. Quite a number — even of the dancers — were alone and I did not once see a male and female dance, as we do, in couples.

Some of the dresses would not have disgraced a masked ball; the shapes of the hats worn were very interesting and the effect of them was fine. A few of the tallest hats were surmounted by little Union Jacks.

Many of the dresses were variations on Panataloon, and not the least remarkable thing about them being the choice of colours displayed. The combinations were not only striking and original but often quite beautiful as well.

(From *In a Forgotten Colony*, 1917.)

The element of parody described by Defries is remarkably similar to that noted by Orlando Patterson in the Homowo festival of the West African Ga people. Patterson notes of the festival that "the improvised masks seen in this section [of the procession] are often native caricatures of local European officials." (From *The Sociology of Slavery*, 1973.)

In Junkanoo, the element of parody was not limited to the visual side of the parade; singing also played an important role. The improvised songs which accompanied the rushing were often commentaries on the year's events, and local dignitaries were commonly derided in them. So pointed were they, indeed, that people interviewed sixty years later were reluctant to divulge the words to certain songs, as the victims or their families were still alive.

There were other, more innocuous songs as well. Many of these are still sung today; and the texts of three are presented below.

Scrap Drummer (Mr H. Lee, Nassau)

Mama Bake De Johnny Cake (sung at Christmas)

Chorus

Ma-ma bake de johnny cake,
Christmas comin'.
Ma-ma bake de johnny cake,
Christmas comin'.

Verse

If ya gown too narrow,
Buy half a yard, make it wider.
If ya gown too narrow,
Buy half a yard, make it wider.

Spare Me Another Year O Lord (sung at New Year)

Spare me another year, O Lord.
Spare me another year, O Lord.
Sen' me back to Havana,
Fill me up wid banana,
Spare me another year, O Lord.

A-Rushin' Through De Crowd (sung on both occasions)

A-rushin', a-rushin',
A-rushin' through de crowd,
A-rushin', a-rushin',
A-rushin' through de crowd.

(Three songs transcribed from memory by E.C. Bethel)

It is no accident that two of the three songs transcribed show a marked preoccupation with food, for the years of the First World War brought acute economic hardship to the colony. Although the War's initial effects were negligible in the capital, in the Out Islands the opposite was true. In the south-eastern Bahamas, war with Germany put a stop to the shipping industry, and the islands were plunged into a severe depression. Deprived of their jobs on board ship and access to Central America, many Bahamians in Inagua and Long Cay faced unemployment. The situation was such, in fact, that special War Relief funds had to be dispatched to save those islands from starvation. In consequence, the War years saw the beginning of a massive migration of Out Islanders to Nassau, and by 1917, the capital's resources were being strained to the limit.

It was not until that year, however, that Nassauvians began to feel the worst effects of the War. Until then, in fact, the fortunes of the city had improved somewhat; war in Europe had meant that American attention was being focussed closer to home. The years 1915 and 1916 saw an improvement in the sponge and sisal trades, and tourism, still seasonal, experienced two good winters.

The entry of the United States into the War in April 1917, however, put an end to what little hope of economic recovery the colony might have had. Not only were American markets suddenly closed to foreign goods, but U.S. exports were also severly curtailed. Its main supply of food cut off, the colony was threatened with total economic collapse. So acute was the situation by the end of 1917, that Governor Allardyce was forced to travel to Washington in an effort to secure food for the colony. Some aid was secured, but the following August still brought days when no bread was to be had in the capital; and on the Out Islands, where opposition to the 'white man's war' was strong, the atmosphere was mutinous.

"The signing of the Armistice . . . on 11 November, 1918," writes Dr Gail Saunders, "was met by wild enthusiasm in Nassau and the Out Islands . . . Bells were rung, bunting put

Found Head-dress (private collection)

up, and market women danced in the streets for joy, heads garlanded with flowers." (From *The Social History of The Bahamas, 1890 – 1953*, PhD Disseration, 1985.) Even the Armistice, however, was a cause of worry for the colony's future. One positive aspect of war had been the employment, as soldiers, of some 2,000 young men. The prospect of their return to an economy already plagued with high unemployment was dismaying; and when they arrived in 1919, they found that little had changed. "Poverty," observes Dr Saunders, "still characterised the colony". The future, in spite of peace, looked bleak.

But The Bahamas was once again saved by the intervention of Fate. In December 1919, the Congress of the United States passed an Act which made it illegal for Americans to manufacture, import or sell intoxicating liquors. Prohibition had begun, and with it came an era of prosperity for The Bahamas unrivalled by anything in the colony's past. The export of liquor to thirsty Americans would bring more changes than any event of previous years.

The Volstead Act came into effect in early 1920, and by then the Bahamian bootlegging trade had begun. Nassau warehouses had been filled with American liquor as soon as the passing of the Bill was imminent; and the early 1920s saw a frenzy of activity as Bahamians scrambled to profit from Prohibition. Liquor, supplied by Britain and smuggled through The Bahamas into the United States, brought enormous returns. Desperate for shares of these, people jumped to the task; and every available vessel in Nassau was pressed into service. As the U.S. Coast Guard, in the early years, was no match for the experienced Bahamian seamen, smuggling flourished; fortunes were made overnight, and the entire country profited. Indeed,

> neglected churches were renovated with liquor money, charities were refinanced, life in general took on a splendour and a spaciousness.
>
> (From H.M. Bell, *Bahamas, the Isles of June*, 1936.)

5
'Neeley, Your Rum So Sweet'

Junkanoo in The Bahamas: 1920 – 1933

With Prohibition came massive development for Nassau. The prosperity which accompanied the liquor trade brought employment, modernisation and a higher standard of living, and for the first time in decades the town flourished. The revenue gained from bootlegging peaked as early as 1923, and then gradually declined. But money was not all that liquor brought. By the middle of the decade two new industries, both related to bootlegging, were earning handsome incomes for the Government. So successful were they that they would lay the foundation for a greater, more enduring prosperity; for it is on them that the economy of the modern Bahamas rests. The industries are foreign investment and tourism.

The first, which took the form of the development of real estate, overtook the colony in the mid 1920s. In part an off-shoot of the land boom then sweeping South Florida, its effect on Nassau was to create an energetic new industry. Attracted by several factors, not least among them the ready availability of liquor, North Americans began to spend their winters in The Bahamas. These were followed by eager land developers, who flocked to purchase large tracts of New Providence and Bimini on which to create exclusive residences for wealthy clients. As a result, jobs for surveyors and construction workers abounded. The price of land, hitherto negligible, soared; and with it rose wages. As foreign developers mapped out elegant, segregated neighbourhoods to sell to the rich,

black and white Bahamians continued the land boom 'Over-the-Hill'. Those residents of Grant's Town and Bain Town who were more wealthy than others moved into the new sub-divisions, and recent migrants from the Out Islands, who had come to Nassau in search of work, settled quickly in the vacant homes. Construction was the mark of the new age, and the limits of the city bulged south and west.

At the same time, the tourist trade, active since the 1860s, underwent a significant change. Liquor brought a new type of visitor to the colony, and Nassau swarmed with the fashionable and the newly rich. Some idea of the changing climate of the town may be gained from the writings of two contemporary Americans:

> Bay Street . . . was no longer a sun drenched idle avenue where traffic in sponges and sisal progressed torpidly. It was filled with slit-eyed, hunch shouldered strangers, with a bluster of Manhattan in their voices and a wary truculence of manners.
>
> (From H. Van der Water, *The Real McCoy*, 1933.)

> Up and down streets that buccaneers had laid out rolled a new tide of marked men: bootleggers, gangster leaders, kidnappers, cracksmen, while for contrast there rubbed shoulders with them public school teachers out for a lark and women tourists who never suspected who their passing neighbours might be.
>
> (From H. McLachlan Bell, *Bahamas, Isles of June*, 1936.)

The gangsters were not the only visitors to Nassau; arriving too were members of the 'flapper' generation, seeking cheap liquor and good dancing, as well as representatives of the very rich of all nations. Although some of the more conservative of the Nassau elite longed for a return of the sedate, well-mannered visitor of past years, there was no denying that the new breed of tourist was good for the economy; and by the late 1920s, the active development of tourism was well on its way. By 1929, Nassau had gained a reputation as a popular resort.

Liquor exports, too, continued to bring in money. Despite declining returns, the income from alcohol never fell below £500,000 throughout the 1920s; thus it continued to provide the colony with a solid base of capital until the end of Prohibition. Gone was the poverty of previous years. For the first time in over half a century, money flowed into Nassau. Employment, formerly so scarce, was to be had by all; as Dr Saunders notes in her description of the era, bootlegging provided almost everybody with jobs.

Nassau's harbour was swarming with ships unloading thousands of barrels of liquor from English and Scottish liquor manufacturers. The wharves and streets were soon crowded with barrels and cases of liquor, while women and children were employed to roll barrels off Bay Street to nearby ware-houses, which quickly multiplied.

(From *The Social History of The Bahamas, 1890 – 1953*, 1985.)

Small wonder, then, that Junkanoo developed substantially during the period. As prosperity brought wealth and a growing tolerance for the festival, the parades finally began to assume some of their modern characteristics. For the first time,

Junkanoo Dancer I (Mr and Mrs V. Vanderpool-Wallace, Nassau)

Junkanoo drew spectators to Bay Street, and the festival adjusted itself accordingly. The parades took on the air of public performances; costumes and instruments grew in sophistication; and Junkanoo became more orderly, more spectacular.

It is to Prohibition time that we can trace back the refinement of that art peculiar to Junkanoo — the application of fringed coloured paper to cardboard or cloth to create a costume. During the 1920s, the masqueraders became more concerned with the visual aspect of the parade than before and they had both the means and the incentive to see to its development. As a result, the costumes of the era grew more and more flamboyant, and special care was taken with the preparation of the headdresses. Although the traditional steeple and beehive hats were still very much in evidence, more elaborate figures — animals, birds, flowers, ships and other objects — were now worn on the head. The bodies of the masqueraders, too, were covered in more colourful disguises; and costumes made from fringed tissue paper (later to be replaced by the more versatile crepe paper) supplanted those made from cheap materials such as newspaper, sponge and sacking.

As for the instruments, they demonstrated clearly the changed character and fortunes of the time. Drums once fashioned from empty pork barrels and round cheese containers were now built out of old rum kegs. The conch shells and fog-horns of a simpler, seafaring life were replaced by horns which could be bought in stores — toy horns, bicycle horns, and, for those with enough money, bugles. And no instruments spoke so eloquently of the new age than the 'scrapers', which provided a rhythmic accompaniment to the drums. Traditionally made from anything which, when scraped, would make a satisfactory sound — washboards and spoons, the jawbones of animals and sticks — they were symbols of their times. Just as scrapers of past years had been evidence of poverty, those of the Roaring Twenties demonstrated the colony's new-found prosperity. The 'bottle and nail', for instance, which began to replace the washboard, was undeniably related to the liquor trade; the bottle in question, whose corrugated sides were raked to provide a rhythm, was generally one which had contained Gilbey's Gin. Similarly, the saw, played with a nail, knife or screwdriver, soon took precedence over the jawbone, and was emblematic of the construction boom.

The Junkanoos continued to sing as they paraded, and the songs they produced, like the instruments they carried, were representative of the age. At least one of these songs, not unnaturally, celebrated the new-found liquor prosperity:

Neeley, Your Rum So Sweet

Neeley, your rum so sweet,
Neeley, your rum so sweet,
Neeley, your rum so sweet,
Neeley, your rum so sweet.

(Collected by E.C. Bethel, Nassau, September 3rd, 1976.)

Local preachers were scandalised by the song, for it was obviously based on a favourite church anthem, "Jesus, Your Name So Sweet". Blasphemous it may have been, but it also provided a succinct commentary on the era. Mr Neeley was the owner-operator of 'The Weary Willies', a dance hall and drinking house situated Over-the-Hill. The advent of American business to Nassau had made the segregation of Bay Street establishments mandatory; consequently, bars like Mr Neeley's sprang up in the coloured areas of town. The tribute paid to Mr Neeley's rum was not only symptomatic of a lack of regard for traditional moral norms. It was also, in its simple way, indicative of the increasing racism of the decade.

Another song popular with those who 'rushed' recounted the burning of the old Hotel Colonial. That hotel, built at the end of the nineteenth century, was a wooden structure on the edge of Nassau, not far from the homes and businesses of blacks and whites alike. When the fire started in the hotel's laundry room on the morning of March 31st, 1922, it was quick to spread; and fire-fighters worked, with limited resources, to save the houses nearby. Water was scarce, equipment faulty, and the fire only stopped by explosives; miraculously, no lives were lost. The hotel was destroyed, however, and damages amounted to a quarter of a million pounds.

Do A'Nanny

Chorus

Do a'nanny, do a'nanny,
Do a'nanny, how ya do?
Eh-eh, do a'nanny, do.

1 Oh, de hotel bu'n down smack an' smooth
De white man run an' he lef his shoes.
Eh-eh, do a'nanny, do. **Chorus**

2 De hotel bu'n down to de groun'
No more dancin' in dis town.
Eh-eh, do a'nanny, do. **Chorus**

3 Dere was a woman who thought it safer
To bring out all of her tissue paper.
Eh-eh, do a'nanny, do. **Chorus**

4 Dey use de water from de swimmin' pool
Das how dey save de Central School.
Eh-eh, do a'nanny, do. **Chorus**

5 Dey try dey bes' to put fire out
But de hose it burs' an' wouldn't spout.
Eh-eh, do a'nanny, do. **Chorus**

6   When de fire was at its height
De Commandant sen' for dynamite.
Eh-eh, do a'nanny, do. **Chorus**

(First verse transcribed from memory by E.C. Bethel. Words for additional verses from Nassau informant, April 3rd, 1977.)

It is appropriate that the popular satirists of the day should have seen fit to compose such a long and enduring song — the refrain is still sung today — about the Colonial fire, for the aftermath of that event was to affect the colony for some time. The Government, faced with the daunting prospect of providing accommodation for the next tourist season, scrambled to find a builder for a new hotel. In the early summer, an agreement was signed with a subsidiary of the Munson Steamship Company, and work on the New Colonial began at once. Plans for the new hotel included its being larger than any structure then existing in the colony; it was made entirely of concrete; and, most formidable, it was to be completed in a total of six months.

Bahamians, skilled and unskilled alike, converged on the building site in search of jobs. What they did not expect was the Munson Company's determination to import much of its labour. Almost half the force which began work on the New Colonial that summer was Cuban. Bahamian labourers had to be satisfied with menial, poorly paid jobs. If this were not enough, the Cubans went on strike shortly after they arrived, in protest at bad conditions. Their demands were quickly granted, but no concessions were made to Bahamian employees. During the rest of the summer and all of autumn, therefore, tensions between the two groups ran high. These culminated in a near-riot on the construction site on December 4th, which brought work to a halt.

Alarmed by the possibility of not meeting its deadline, the Munson Company took prompt action. Fifty-five Cubans were sent back to Havana, and the Bahamian workers placated; shortly thereafter, work resumed. The hotel was finished on schedule, and the New Colonial admitted its first visitors in February 1923.

The Bahamians, however, did not go unpunished for their part in the fight. On December 21st, the *Nassau Guardian* published the following notice:

No Suspension of Street Nuisance Rules

We are informed that it has been decided by the Governor in Council not to suspend this year the Street Nuisance Rules as is customary during certain hours of the Christmas season. This decision will, we are sure, meet with the approval of the community and will be welcomed by those who have long wished for the abolition of this extraordinary manner of celebrating Christmas.

And the *Guardian* of December 26th noted that:

although an attempt was made by some irrepressible youngsters to come into Bay Street in the early hours of [Christmas] morning the Police, with the assistance of the hose from the fire engines, kept them at bay.

The matter of the Colonial Hotel did not end there. The hotel which opened in 1923 was typical of the age; it was ostentatious, modern, and it flaunted its American ties. From the beginning it was apparent that the Munson Company intended to run it along the strictest lines. Within its walls was enforced the kind of racial discrimination hitherto only known to those Bahamians who had visited the United States. So rigid were its racial policies that for the first two years after it opened all employees were brought in from Miami. Not until 1925 were Bahamians permitted to apply for jobs in the hotel; and black Bahamians were prohibited from using its facilities until racial segregation was outlawed in 1956. For the first twenty-odd years of its existence, the New Colonial Hotel was a symbol of racism in The Bahamas.

The banning of Junkanoo, Christmas 1922 aside, was not a common practice during the early years of Prohibition. Prosperity and the fascination of visitors with the festival helped make Junkanoo an anticipated part of a Bahamian Christmas. Both the authorities and the press, after their early ambivalence, were inclined to look favourably on the parade. In fact, the *Nassau Guardian* of December 26th, 1922, in its report on the abortive Christmas festivities, advocated that Junkanoo be allowed to take place on New Year's Day:

> From all accounts there was considerable harmless merry-making 'Over the hill' . . . some concessions should be made, we think, on New Year's Day, when no exception could be taken to a properly organised carnival in a suitable place. There is far too little innocent amusement provided for our people and it is only fair that their spirits should have an outlet on occasions.

And the *Tribune* on December 26th of the following season reported:

> Xmas passed very quietly. The masqueraders . . . behaved themselves very well . . . Although the government permitted them to come 'to the market' the men remained 'Over the hill' for the reason that the government refused to allow them in the city last year.

That paper seemed very supportive of the masqueraders in question, and was quick to realise the political and economic power inherent in the group. The above report continued:

The stores in the city did practically no business. The stores

Super Star (Mr and Mrs W. Saunders, Nassau)

in Grants Town reaped a golden harvest. Many of the shop-keepers in the city, when they learnt of the intention of the 'boys' to remain in Grant [sic] Town offered the leaders money to change their plan but they . . . refused the bribe. The 'boys' say they intend to develop their own district.

And an editorial in the same issue of the *Tribune*, written by L. Gilbert Dupuch, observed that:

as insignificant as the action of the masquerades in refusing to come to the 'market' may appear, it marks a distinct development in the people and reveals a spirit of democracy and unity that has been unknown in The Bahamas formerly . . . the people throughout The Bahamas are waking up and, like the masquerades, so will the electors have changed at the upcoming general elections. We are proud to see the people independent even in the small things. We can now hope for a great change in the personnel of the House of Assembly not so far distant.

Dupuch was not far wrong. The action of the junkanoos in 1923 and the reaction of the Bay Street merchants illustrated the power wielded by the working people in an era when cash was plentiful. For that reason as well as any other, the government of the 1920s was kindly disposed towards Junkanoo, and so facilitated its growth.

The expansion of the tourist industry during this period, however, was perhaps the single greatest asset to the development of Junkanoo. By 1923, the Bahamian public was well aware of the benefits of tourism, and the government determined to make Nassau the most popular resort in the region. The hard work was not in vain. "By 1929," writes Dr Saunders,

Nassau was well established as a resort, owing to its unrivalled winter climate, fine bathing beaches, fishing, yachting, tennis, golf, and its 'old-world atmosphere'. Additionally, the government during the 1920s adopted a more aggressive policy towards 'selling' The Bahamas. The Development Board . . . spent thousands of pounds in advertisements, maps, books and pamphlets to attract wealthy Americans and Canadians. The Government made sure that adequate facilities were available. Sporting activities such as lawn tennis flourished . . . Frequent tournaments were held on first class grass courts, either at the exclusive white-only Nassau Lawn Tennis Club or at the hotels, which had the same racial policy. Golf links were built at Fort Charlotte and at the recently completed Bahamas Country Club at Cable beach. Duck shooting took place from November to April at the two New Providence Lakes . . . and wild pigeon shooting could also be enjoyed during the winter months. Fishing trips could be arranged and sea-bathing was popular on the white coral sand at Hog Island.

Guests were ensured accommodation in the major hotels — the New Colonial, the Fort Montagu . . . and the more traditional Royal Victoria. There were also smaller hotels . . . There were several boarding houses and some private families accepted paying guests. Some tourists leased furnished houses for the winter . . .

Attracted by the knowledge that liquor was available in Nassau, 'tourists came in by waves and floods'.

(From *Social History*, 1985.)

Competition from Bermuda spurred the Development Board (the body responsible for promoting the colony to the tourists) to emphasise, among other things, those practices which distinguished Nassau from other places. Junkanoo, despite its poor early reputation, was not excepted, and was advertised along with the colony's natural assets. That Junkanoo should suddenly be viewed so favourably by the authorities and the press — the very people who, in previous years, condemned it — is no great mystery. Prosperity and employment had brought order to Junkanoo, and the parades were beginning to resemble floor-shows rather than melées.

It must not be forgotten, either, that during this same period in the United States the cultural development of the Afro-American was being encouraged by the rich and sophisticated. Spurred on by the spread of Cubism, whose followers looked to Africa for the inspiration of their art, a number of wealthy American liberals had become patrons of Black culture. It is debatable whether they accepted or even understood the radical implications of the movement they supported. Nevertheless, the Roaring Twenties were years during which the promotion of Negro culture — be it music, writing, or art — was fashionable. They were the Jazz years, the Garvey years, the years of Langston Hughes and Claude McKay, years when, for whites, excursions to exotic places such as Harlem and Haiti were in vogue. It is no wonder, then, that the American visitors to Nassau regarded Junkanoo with interest.

In 1925, action was taken by the authorities to ensure that the parade continue to grow in a seemly fashion. In conjunction with the Development Board, therefore, private individuals, interested in maintaining the orderly aspect of the parades, offered awards for the participants.

> With the object of popularising the quaint custom of masquerading on New Year's morning the Development Board has decided to give £25 in prizes for competitors judged to be wearing the best costume.
>
> (From the *Nassau Guardian*, December 10th, 1925.)

It is interesting to note that, in the promotion of the parade by the government of the 1920s, emphasis was always placed on the visual aspect of the festival. The prizes were to be given for the best costume only, the music of Junkanoo being dismissed as little more than 'noise'. Indeed, in the plans to organise the parade, the Development Board made arrangements to provide 'real' music for the participants:

> Though in past years the John Canoes ... have always attracted interest, the display on next New Year's morning is likely to surpass all previous ones ...
>
> The Commandant of Police has kindly consented to allow the Police Band to head the procession.
>
> (From the *Nassau Guardian*, December 19th, 1925.)

The further organisation of the festival was encouraged as the urge to turn Junkanoo into a spectacle for tourists grew. By 1928, Junkanoo was being hailed as a native Bahamian custom, a fine example of primitive African ritual, and an asset to the tourist trade. That year even saw an attempt at associating the Christmas festival with a pre-Lenten celebration; in March, masqueraders were asked to take part in the Mi Careme Carnival organised for the visitors. A description of that parade, held on Friday, March 23rd, 1928, between 9 and 12 p.m., gives us an idea of the face of the festival during the bootleg era.

John Canoe Parade

A grand display of fireworks, roman candles, rockets and flares opened the parade and continued through the early stages. The judges' float was parked in the middle of Bay street, opposite the Club [i.e. the Old Colony Club, upstairs above the present-day Nassau shop, between Charlotte and Market Streets], and proved the centre of activities, as the John Canoes, clanking their cow bells, blowing horns, and pounding drums, danced and paraded and caracoled [i.e. danced making half turns] up and down the street from one end to the other.

Dense throngs of spectators lined the street on both sides, as well as the sidewalks, and the John Canoes had considerable difficulty in making their way through the crowd. Premature

Thatch Palm Head-dress (Shell Bahamas Ltd)

explosions of fireworks, however, occasionally made an abrupt clearing in the street.

During the height of the pandemonium, the judging took place, and the John Canoes performed their wildest antics in front of the judges' float. Special flares were lighted, and a spotlight from the balcony of The Club was trained on the scene, while a Paramount News camera man took motion pictures from a nearby roof.

The winner of the £10 first prize was covered with red, white and blue streamers. As a hat, he wore an elaborately constructed aeroplane, with the Union Jack on each wing and "Carnival Week," in bold letters, on each side of the fuselage . . . Second prize was won by a costume of streamers, with a huge roof of streamers for a hat. The third prize was given to two John Canoes covered from head to foot with Spanish Moss. Fourth prize was taken by Father Christmas, a much beribboned individual with a huge fringed headpiece. On the front of the hat was a portrait of Father Christmas and on the reverse was the announcement, "Xmas Gifts for All." Other prize winners included a black skeleton-like horse's head, wearing a most fiendish expression . . . Another was a dancing girl, and others wore streamer costumes. One white ghost, something on the cubist idea, paraded up and down with black horns sticking out of its head, and hands on the end of sticks. Another good costume was the huge fat man in burlap who cavorted wildly around. Several bridal couples, with and without a best man, ran here and there.

The parade, although not as successful as the annual Christmas and New Year John Canoe shows, was greatly enjoyed by the many tourists who witnessed it, none of whom had ever seen anything of the sort before.

(From the *Nassau Guardian*, March 24th, 1928)

This positive attitude of the press, like the prosperity of the age, was not to last. By the final years of the 1920s despite appearances, the Bahamian economy was failing. The decline in Bahamian fortunes between 1926 and 1933 is reflected in changes in Junkanoo; and as the economic situation worsened, the tolerance for the parades faded.

A series of hurricanes — one in 1926, three in 1928, and particularly devastating storms in 1929 and 1932 — hit the colony, draining the Government's resources and rendering many people homeless, particularly in the Out Islands and Over-the-Hill. It is no surprise, therefore, that the Junkanoo parade of Christmas 1929 was prohibited. Again, however, the merchants on Bay Street, whose custom it was during Prohibition to open their shops on Christmas Day, felt the absence of Junkanoo almost as much as the paraders themselves, and the end of 1930 saw them petitioning the government to allow the festival to take place. That year's Christmas parade, though, was a disappointment. "The celebrations were only half hearted," reported the *Guardian* (December 27th, 1930); and an editorial in the *Tribune* that year noted that:

Masquerading is dying by degrees. This Christmas not one costume with any point to it was to be seen 'in the market'. It is a great pity that this celebration cannot be restored to its former colourful brilliance . . . Ten years ago in Nassau masquerading was a distinct art. Today it lacks both point and colour, and has nothing to justify its existence.

(From the *Tribune*, December 27th, 1930.)

The following years were little better. The Wall Street Crash of October 1929 brought foreign investment in real estate to a halt; and although land prices remained high, economic development stood still. Tourism, too, suffered. As fewer and fewer Americans could afford winters abroad, Nassau's seasonal income fell.

Son Rise (Shell Bahamas Ltd)

The optimism of the 1920s, however, was slow to die. Despite everything, Nassau still had one asset: liquor. Although the peak of the bootlegging era was long past, the government continued to glean revenue from re-exports of alcohol, and those Americans who were not yet affected by the Depression continued to visit the city. The Development Board, finding that tourists could no longer afford to spend the winter months in Nassau, sought salvation in trippers; and the early 1930s saw the engagement of cruise ships to call at Nassau. The reports of the Junkanoo parade of Christmas 1932 seem to illustrate the persistent feeling among Bahamians that the bad times were only temporary, and, if weathered, would lead to better:

> The traditional Christmas parade of masquerades was held yesterday morning [i.e. on Boxing Day — in 1932, Christmas fell on a Sunday], Bay Street being crowded with Johnnie Canoes and spectators. There were more masquerades than last year.
>   Tourists from the Munargo landed just at the end of the parade, passengers from other excursion ships landing afterwards.
>
>   (From the *Tribune,* December 27th, 1932.)

Even so, the *Guardian*'s description of the same parade cannot disguise the growing hardship of the age. "Although the usual cow bells, horns and drums were much in evidence," writes that journal,

> There were few who were dressed up. Several of the old time tall hats could be seen and quite a few good costumes were noticeable but the standard of masquerading seems to be deteriorating each year.
>
>   (From the *Nassau Guardian,* December 28th, 1932)

The final blow to the economy, however, had yet to be dealt. As long as Prohibition remained in effect, the colony did not want for income. Yet even that blessing was soon to end. As Michael Craton observes in his 1986 *History of The Bahamas:*

> [The wealth of the 1920s] was a brittle affluence and was destined to vanish as swiftly as it had arrived. [As long as] Prohibition was still in force, there was always a steady, if declining, inward flow of money. Only upon the repeal of Prohibition by the Twenty-First Amendment in the first year of Franklin D. Roosevelt's first term as President [1933] did the source dry up [and] the years between the Twenty-First Amendment and the American entry into the Second World War in December, 1941, were a tale of savage depression in The Bahamas, made none the more bearable by its familiarity.

Prohibition, despite its material benefits, had created a society ill-equipped for depression. Out Island development had been neglected, traditional industries allowed to fall into ruin, and the recent hurricanes had threatened the livelihood of many. Sponging and agriculture were suffering, whole settlements had been demolished, and starvation once again seemed imminent. During the early 1930s, large sums of money would be allocated for Out Island relief, draining the colony's reserves, and the tide of migrants from the Out Islands to the capital swelled once more. The party was over; it was time to return to work.

6
'Burma Road Declare War on da Conchy Joe'

Junkanoo in The Bahamas: 1933 – 1947

The decade of the 1930s witnessed the growth and development of tourism and foreign investment in Nassau [which] primarily benefitted the white *nouveau riche* mercantile and professional class in Nassau . . . as the gap between rich and poor . . . grew wider, discriminating politics grew more severe, causing an increase in racial tensions and consciousness.

(From Dr Gail Saunders,*The social History of The Bahamas, 1890-1953*, 1985.)

It is difficult to examine the evolution of Junkanoo in the post-Prohibition era without also considering the corresponding activities of the black Bahamian during the same period. On the surface, Junkanoo did not improve at all. Rather, it seemed to regress, grow more disorderly and uncivilised, until it was banned altogether by the government in 1942. It was not until the reinstatement of the parade in 1947 that anything like development appeared to take place in the festival; yet once begun, it never failed. One cannot, therefore, dismiss the decades following Prohibition as times during which Junkanoo deteriorated. On the contrary, beneath the apparent stagnation of the festival, some development must have occurred which would account for its rapid growth half a generation after it went into decline.

To a student of West Indian history, the idea that the 1930s were a decade of radical social change is by no means new.

Indeed, when considering the 1930s in any British West Indian colony, one must take into account two main factors — poverty and the growth of the labour movement. As Dr Saunders notes in her dissertation:

[In the British Caribbean] the depression of the 1930s fostered the growth of the trade union movement, and coincided with the rise of the party system and growth of national consciousness. Economic distress, poverty and discontent caused an explosion of strikes and riots throughout the British West Indies.

The Bahamas was both like and unlike the West Indian model. The 1930s, in contrast with the previous decade, brought unemployment and unrest to the Bahamian workers. Yet these hard times did not provoke the development of any coherent labour movement in the islands, nor did they pave the way for the rise of any black leader of note. As the colony emerged from the War years, it appeared to be decades behind its neighbours in terms of social reform, so much so that the historian Gordon Lewis felt justified in observing that "the Atlantic West Indies [Bermuda and The Bahamas] entered the modern period politically antiquated, culturally depressed and psychologically retarded." (*The Growth of the Modern West Indies*, 1968.)

Much has been made of the apparent placidity of the

Scrap Dancer with Cowbells II (private collection)

Bahamian worker during an era of protest. Michael Craton, author of *A History of The Bahamas*, attributes it in part to the provision of jobs, during the early 1930s, by the extensive

land development of the Canadian investor Sir Harry Oakes, and in part to the War effort of the early forties. In *The Story of The Bahamas*, Dr Paul Albury notes that Bahamians were traditionally used to hard times:

> . . . certain and steady employment, large savings, investments in stocks and bank mortgages were unknown to the great majority of the Bahamian people [who] could fall from no great height because they had not climbed very far.

Economic difficulties were offset by the revival in 1936 of the salt industry in Inagua and the recording, in 1937, of ''the best tourist season in history''. Gordon Lewis, however, is far less generous, maintaining that the inactivity of the Bahamian workers was due to the fact that the colony was founded ''on parasitic forms of wealth, racial apartheid, political apathy and economic *laissez-faire*.'' (Growth, 1968.) Among historians, then, it has long been the practice to assert that the Bahamian labourers were slow to protest, and, indeed, apathetic towards the possibility of positive social change.

In her dissertation, however, Dr Saunders notes that Bahamian labour unrest did exist during the 1930s.

> The majority of the black labouring population . . . suffering from many hardships and from the growing unemployment, became increasingly restless. Two isolated incidents, one in New Providence, and the other at Inagua, demonstrated that discontent was far from uncommon in The Bahamas.

A survey of the Junkanoo parades of the post-Prohibition era illustrates her point. The workers' restlessness was evident in the festival and as the years passed, reports of disorderly conduct by masqueraders grew more frequent. By Christmas

1933, the *Tribune* reported that the parades had become gathering places for "increasing numbers of men who are not masqueraders, but who ... are ... drunk and carrying menacing sticks that they do not hesitate to use" (December 27th), and the next year noted that "a number of men, who are not masqueraders, came to town drunk and started trouble right away." (December 26th, 1934.)

What was missing, however, was a coherent workers' movement to make its needs known. One is reminded of the Bahamian slave society of a century before, when the isolation of the islands made it difficult for the slaves to organise any substantial uprising against their masters. In the 1930s, although more of the population was centred in New Providence, a similar situation existed. It is significant that the two disturbances which did occur took place in Nassau and Inagua — two communities which were traditionally more urbanised than the rest of the archipelago.

Geography was not the only factor inhibiting the growth of a Bahamian labour movement during this time. Also acting against unity was the fact that Bahamian workers were employed in many different areas. Those on the Out Islands were farmers, fishermen, spongers and boatmen. In Inagua, the majority of the population worked in the salt industry; and in New Providence, tourism created many winter jobs, and construction took care of the summers. Nassauvians were taxi drivers, hotel workers, musicians, nightclub operators, businessmen, carpenters, masons, plumbers, teachers, lawyers, domestics and tailors. Although the early years of the decade saw the formation of many self-help societies and cooperatives, the workers were always divided by occupation. Other West Indian societies, with their broad agricultural and industrial bases, found it easier to develop unified labour movements.

It would be a mistake to conclude, as some have done, that the Bahamian masses were either apathetic or placid. On the contrary; the 1930s brought with them more tensions than the colony had experienced to date. For the first time, Nassau was faced with serious overcrowding in the black areas of the city, and as more and more Out Islanders arrived in the capital, the problem grew worse. Wages were low, unemployment chronic, and opportunities for work outside the colony were scarce. Dr Paul Albury observes in his *Story of The Bahamas* that:

> No longer were there outlets for employment abroad. United States immigration restrictions prevented Bahamians from working in that country, and the stevedore and contract labour business of the south-eastern islands ... had dried up. Bahamians were confined to The Bahamas, so to speak, and whatever could be made of their lives had to be made there.

Significantly, for the first time, the poverty which had hit the colony was blatantly uneven. For the majority of Bahamians, the Depression brought hard times; but for a handful, it provided more opportunities for the making of money. The 1930s were seeing the rise of a small, white, wealthy class, which flourished while the majority of the population grew poorer.

Gordon Lewis notes about the aftermath of the boom years in Bermuda and The Bahamas that:

> the ultimate beneficiaries ... were, first, the foreign commercial agents ... and, second, [members of the dominant] merchant class whose brief, lucrative careers ... provided the financial foundations of their status as the social and political ruling class ... For the island masses it was all, at best, a brief and illusory prosperity.
>
> (From *The Growth of the Modern West Indies,* 1968.)

In the 1930s the white merchant classes continued to amass wealth, from the exploitation of land and the tax-free nature of the colony's economy. Inspired by Harold Christie, a white Bahamian who realised that the hard times could be the colony's greatest asset, they began inviting to The Bahamas wealthy North Americans. These men, though unaffected by the stock market crash, were nevertheless being squeezed by their governments' new taxation laws, and were eager for profitable investment; for them, The Bahamas was paradise. The effort paid off. In 1934, Harold Christie "achieved a minor triumph . . . he managed to attract to The Bahamas as a resident and huge investor the richest citizen of [Canada] — Mr, later Sir, Harry Oakes." (Michael Craton, *A History of The Bahamas*, 1986.)

It was a brilliant move. Oakes was not only good for the government's coffers; he also provided a number of Bahamian workers with much-needed jobs. It is possible, as has already been mentioned, that by so doing, he managed to diffuse, for a time, the growing labour tensions of the age.

> Oakes bought up more than 7,000 acres in New Providence alone, [and] with the enthusiasm of a young man he threw himself into ambitious projects costing . . . over $400,000 and employing many local labourers who had been on the point of starvation.
>
> (From Michael Craton, *A History of The Bahamas*, 1986.)

One should not underestimate the values of Oakes' generosity in a time of unrest. By the mid 1930s, as reports of Junkanoo indicate, poverty had reached a post-War low. In 1934, "the costumes worn [in the festival] were more or less

Junkanoo Dancer II (Mr G. Trotman, Nassau)

disgraceful" (*Guardian*, January 2nd, 1937), and by 1935, reports of crime and violence, both within and without the parade, were common. So welcome were the jobs Oakes provided that, although he died in 1943, his popularity continued well into the 1970s. Of him, Dame Doris Johnson, chronicler of the Progressive Liberal Party's rise to power, writes:

> His building projects kept almost two thousand Bahamian labourers contentedly employed at fair wages and soon made him one of the most popular men in Nassau. Only four years after his arrival he was elected to the House of Assembly; he hobnobbed with the Royal Governor, and was made a member of the Legislative Council.
>
> (From *The Quiet Revolution in The Bahamas*, 1972.)

Oakes' philanthropy, however, was little more than a stop-gap; the "fair wages" he paid his workers, while higher than the legal minimum, were nevertheless only five shillings a day. As a means of maintaining the colony's stability, it was fated to fall through. What was most significant about Sir Harry Oakes and his ilk was that they had money and ordinary Bahamians did not, and that they were white, and the majority of Bahamians were black.

Against the growing prosperity of the white minority, the majority suffered. Many opportunities formerly available to black Bahamians were, for various reasons, being circumscribed. Gains in business, education and politics were being reversed, and as a result, the black majority was growing increasingly restless.

To begin with, while white businessmen flourished, many black entrepreneurs lost capital during the Depression. As the 1930s progressed, the few blacks who had concerns on Bay Street were edged out. In education, too, inequalities became more pronounced. In 1925, the first Government High School had been opened in the colony, allowing blacks a chance at a secondary education. In 1931, however, the Dundas Civic Centre, a school for hotel workers, was established with the support of the white members of the House of Assembly. To them, it seemed useless to educate blacks for positions which they could not hope to attain; much better to train them for the jobs which were available. In 1934, therefore, faced with a decline in revenue, the House proposed the closure of Government High. The suggestion provoked an uproar in the community, and the school was saved by the fact that its examination results for 1934 were the best in the colony. The damage, however, was done. The fact that the colony's leaders thought so little of a high school for its people rankled; now more than ever, blacks were determined to educate themselves.

The 1930s also witnessed the growth of segregation in Nassau. Part of the reason behind this was, not surprisingly, the rise in American investment in the colony and the continued promotion of tourism. Most of the hotels in Nassau pursued strict discriminatory policies. Although black Bahamians were permitted, after 1925, to work as servants in the hotels, they were allowed to hold no other jobs. Black musicians, for instance, with rare exceptions, were barred; and during the season, whole bands were imported from abroad. So strict was the discrimination that if black Bahamian musicians "wished to hear a foreign orchestra, they had to seek special permission to enter the outside premises and were allowed to listen at the windows." (Saunders, *Social History*, 1985.) The same rules did not, of course, apply to whites; the most successful Bahamian musician of the time was Charles Lofthouse, a white man, the son of a Bay Street merchant.

In politics, too, black Bahamians were growing more and more impotent. By the end of the 1920s, almost a third of

Glitter and Fringe (Mr and Mrs W. Wong, Nassau)

the Bahamian House of Assembly had consisted of black members. In the 1935 elections, however, faced with financial difficulties and a corrupt system, those men lost ground. Of the nine incumbent black members of the House no more than four were returned.

The black population was less able to find a legitimate forum in which to air its views. It could no longer rely on the press to support its cause. The *Tribune* had traditionally been quick to take the part of the labouring population, as evidenced by L. Gilbert Dupuch's editorial on the masqueraders' boycotting of Bay Street at Christmas in 1923. But as it became more prosperous and influential, it also became more conservative. By 1934, its reports on Junkanoo, rather than presenting the masqueraders' social and economic situations, concentrated largely on their behaviour and costumes. An editorial from that year provides evidence of the paper's new attitude towards Junkanoo. Rather than a positive community force, it is portrayed as the remnant of a primitive past which would be better forgotten — a sure betrayal of the people's attitude towards the parade.

> The falling off in John Canoeing represents a change in outlook by the bulk of the population, indicating that . . . the people are developing a greater sense of pride and self-respect. They very properly feel that they should not make a poppy-show of themselves for the entertainment of the public . . . fifteen years ago . . . boys of all classes . . . took part in the celebration and many of them spent months preparing their costumes. It was a wild but spectacular show. Today . . . it is . . . only a vulgar exhibition.
>
> (From the *Tribune*, December 26th, 1934.)

In the course of a decade, the paper had succeeded in setting itself apart from the general population. It occasionally supported the views of the majority, but was not above abandoning those views if they differed from its own. It is interesting that Etienne Dupuch, editor of the Tribune in the 1930s, attributed the decline of masquerading to the simple maturing of the masses. For him, the reason behind the parade's decline was that black Bahamians were growing up, and were likely soon to leave their more primitive habits behind. More and more his paper was assuming the traditional position of the black middle classes. For him, as for them, Junkanoo had no intrinsic value; it was important only because it allowed the lower classes a chance, at Christmas, to let off steam, and for the number of tourists it could attract.

The discontent of the black Bahamians was evident in Junkanoo, and the parades of the era grew increasingly disorganised and rough. Part of the reason for the rapid decline of the festival was the widespread availability of liquor — the most enduring bequest of Prohibition to the ordinary Bahamian. Liquor merchants, many of them newly rich from the export of alcohol to the United States, found themselves with large stocks of spirits and no external market; so they sold their supplies to Bahamians. The price of liquor dropped. By the middle of the decade, "a pint of rum," according to Dr Saunders, "could be purchased for a shilling, slightly more than a loaf of bread, and less than a quart of milk." (*Social History*, 1985.) In consequence, the rate of drunkenness in the capital soared.

During the early 1920s, when alcohol and money had flowed side by side, rum had been the symbol of prosperity. As the years passed, however, it became an emblem of despair, and as times grew worse, reports of drunkenness and fighting during Junkanoo grew more frequent. It should be noted that the invaders of the parades of 1933 and 1934 were not only armed but drunk as well, and that in the latter year, the Commandant of Police "had more fighting drunks to contend with during the Christmas celebrations than on any previous year since he first came to Nassau." (*Tribune,* December 26th, 1934.)

Unemployment, too, played its part. By 1935, jobs for the ordinary Bahamian were so scarce that the simple task of hiring workers had become a risky one for employers. When restoration began that year at Fort Charlotte, eight hundred workers applied for forty positions. And in July 1935, when over four hundred men were informed that only a few openings were available at the site of the new Prince George Hotel, a mini-riot ensued. Small wonder, then, that Junkanoo was growing rowdier.

At first, the government and the press reacted to the decline in the appearance of the parade with remarkable complacency. Instead of recognising that the shoddiness of the celebration was an indication of poverty, the government attempted to restore the festival to its former glory. In December 1933, for instance, concerned with the maintenance of the tourist trade, the Development Board organised a special parade to appeal to visitors; as with the 1928 Mi Careme Carnival, regulations were created to streamline the festival and make it appealing to foreigners.

Plans for New Year's Masquerade
Mummers and Old Style Paraders
Effort to Revive Johnnie Canoes

There will be two classes of paraders — the Mummers, who will wear large head-dresses specially imported by the Development Board, and Old Fashioned Johnnie Canoe Paraders, who will stage an organised attempt to revive the old-style costumes, with their wealth of colour and fringe and to get rid of the drab bagging costumes which have been so prevalent in recent years.

The S.S. *Majestic* is due to arrive at Nassau with 800 passengers on New Year's Day, and arrangements are being made to enable the visitors to see the parade which has tentatively been arranged to start at 8 a.m.

(From the *Tribune,* December 19th, 1933.)

The public, too, tried to maintain the festival as it had been. In 1933, immediately following the end of Prohibition, a voluntary committee, its members drawn from a cross-section of civic-minded Bahamians, was formed to encourage participation in the parades. This committee, following the example of the Development Board in 1925, raised funds by public subscription so that cash prizes could be offered for the best costumes in various categories. Again, the effort was made primarily to promote the tourist trade; like the Mummers' Parade of 1933, however, it was only marginally successful. In December 1934, in recognition of Junkanoo's decline, the *Tribune* carried an editorial, already mentioned, entitled "The Disappearing Johnnie Canoe":

The John Canoe parade 'in the market' yesterday morning was, to say the least, disappointing, perhaps the only costume with any definite point being a life-size [Coca-Cola] bottle sent out by the Sunshine Bottling Co . . .

The Development Board advertises the John Canoes as an attraction at Nassau . . . On several occasions the . . . Board has offered prizes . . . But, in spite of all their efforts, the show has become gradually worse each year. It is now almost intolerable.

An effort should be made by the Board to restore John Canoeing to its former originality and picturesqueness, and this will be possible only if the merchants in the city take an interest in the event. [With their help] the New Year's parade could eventually be developed into a creditable carnival show.

(From the *Tribune,* December 26th, 1934.)

Significantly, no one thought to address the problem of the

deterioration of the parade at its roots — the welfare of the Bahamian workers. No connection was made between the shortage of housing Over-the-Hill and the preponderance of burlap bagging ('crocus sack') in the parades of the thirties, nor between the rising rate of unemployment and the belligerence of the paraders.

It may seem a little odd that the desire for a vibrant Junkanoo parade did not inspire a corresponding interest in the welfare of the people responsible for putting on the show; but in fact, the aim of preserving the parade was strictly mercenary. When the liquor industry collapsed, Bahamian investors immediately turned their attention to the continued exploitation of tourism, and Junkanoo was valued only in so far as it was a spectacle, a quaint but colourful remnant of primitive native ritual. As long as the parade was attractive, then, attention was paid to it; but as soon as it ceased to please the public, it was considered a nuisance, and curtailed.

The masqueraders, however, were not intending to please the public. For them, Junkanoo was still a celebration; but as times grew harder, and they had fewer things to celebrate, it also provided them with an annual forum for airing grievances. The growing unrest of the 1930s' Junkanoo parades can be viewed as political as well as financial, and may be seen to contain, to a limited extent, the Bahamian parallel to the West Indian riots taking place at that time.

As the decade progressed and times grew worse, public opinion about the parade changed. From a quaint custom and a tourist attraction it quickly regained its status as a public nuisance; and, despite the work of the Junkanoo Committee, efforts to curtail the parade were renewed.

The first of these was an attempt to ban the Christmas festival altogether. Church authorities had for decades been complaining that the Junkanoo celebrations interfered with Christmas church services. Defries had noted this as early as 1916, when she wrote:

> At eight o'clock the people began to scatter, but all day long in all the streets you might meet detachments of them and hear the strange beat of their bells and drums, while in the churches negro voices rose on the air singing in unison Christian hymns!

(From Amelia Defries, *In A Forgotton Colony*, 1917.)

The church leaders were not alone in their sentiment. Throughout the early 1900s, both newspapers had advocated that the Christmas parade be outlawed. In 1913, the *Tribune* had referred to it as "a horrible incongruous celebration of the Nativity of 'The Prince of Peace' "; and even during Prohibition, with the support for Junkanoo at its peak, the press continued to favour a New Year's parade over the celebration at Christmas.

> We have always been opposed to the masquerading at Xmas, . . . it is our opinion that there should be either no masquerading or something a little more organised and orderly.

(From the *Tribune*, December 26th, 1923.)

> It is generally felt that Christmas morning is not suitable for the noise and revelling to which the 'John Canoeing' gives rise . . . Yet it would be a pity for this survival of other days to die out, and as it is also celebrated on New Year's Day, it is the masquerade on this day that is to be encouraged.

(From the *Nassau Guardian*, December 10th, 1925.)

> Last year the Governor-in-Council very wisely decided not to suspend the street nuisances regulations at Christmas and the usual masquerading took place on New Year's morning, which is a far more suitable time for this sort of jollification.

(From the *Nassau Guardian*, December 17th, 1930.)

We are pleased to learn that the Board is not supporting any organised parade for Christmas. For years now we have been advocating a quiet Christmas, which is essentially a Christian festival that should not be desecrated by indulging in excesses . . . we can begin to see a time . . . when the whole community will unite in staging a creditable parade on New Year morning and in observing Christmas in a spirit of "peace and goodwill".

(From the *Tribune*, December 20th, 1933.)

By the mid 1930s, public feelings also ran high against the parade. In 1935 a year of disquiet among the labourers, the Christmas parade was banned altogether and the resulting peace was remarked upon:

It was particularly gratifying to the *Guardian* to note that the absence of the John Canoe parade from the city yesterday morning was accompanied by an air of peace and quiet that Bay Street has seldom known at Christmas time.

(From the *Nassau Guardian*, December 26th, 1935.)

Despite all efforts, however, the Christmas parade remained the more popular of the two — a fact which is only fitting, considering the festival's origin in the traditional three-day Christmas holiday. What was more, the season 1936 – 7 saw the arrival of more than four thousand tourists to the colony — the largest number yet — boosting spirits and the economy alike. Not surprisingly, the Junkanoo parade was better than in recent years.

Early yesterday morning the 'John Canoes' were out on Bay Street in force and furnished much amusement to all who retained sufficient consciousness to get out and watch them.

Drummers (private collection)

The object of offering prizes is to encourage more and better costumes to be worn in the parade, which will reflect more credit to Nassau generally. There is no reason why the New Year parade could not become notable for a good appearance instead of notorious for noise.

(From the *Nassau Guardian*, January 2nd, 1937.)

Tourism was on the rise; Junkanoo was popular; some kind of compromise, clearly, was called for. In 1938, then, Boxing Day was also declared a public holiday, and the Junkanoo parade was shifted from Christmas morning to the morning following.

In spite of all these efforts to keep the Junkanoos happy, however, the brief prosperity of 1937 did not last long. The following year, the sponge industry, the one constant source of income for many Out Islanders since the turn of the century, finally failed; a blight had devastated the sponge beds. The poverty of the Out Islands was complete. Again migrants moved to the capital, exacerbating the problems there. Once more tensions ran high, as the following editorial shows:

One of the objectional features of the New Year celebration is that miniature John Canoe Parades *sans* costume or organisation, appear sporadically on busy streets for several days before and after New Year's Day at the imminent risk of stragglers being struck by passing vehicles. Often the spirit of the marchers is a bit truculent and vehicles of all sorts are deliberately impeded . . . Perhaps the phenomenon of the irresistible urge to march to the rhythm of cowbell and tomtom would be of interest to the psychologist, sociologist or just plain tourist but to the average resident it is a bit overdone to put it mildly. The impulse appears too strong to be resisted but, even in a gay holiday season, some courtesy and care is needed in public thoroughfares.

(From the *Nassau Guardian*, December 29th, 1939.)

It has already been noted that the 1930s were, for the rest of the West Indies, an era of labour protest and political solidarity. In The Bahamas, it is possible to view the entire decade of Junkanoo parades as one protest after another. It is interesting, for example, that one of the first changes to take place in the festival was one which recalled the Friendly Society's march to Government Hill in 1890. In 1933, to observe New Year's Day, the Elks' Lodge organised a parade which began and ended Over-the-Hill and which carried the masqueraders through the streets of Nassau, passing Government House on its way.

New Year Torchlight Procession on Monday
''The Elks Band will usher in the New Year with a monster masquerade torchlight procession on Monday night, January 2nd,'' Charles Weir, leader of the band, told the Nassau Daily Tribune yesterday.

. . . ''The ragged brigade, with torches, cowbells, horns, and staves will assemble with the masquerade in the Southern District . . . at 7 p.m. . . . Everyone is invited to bring torches and to decorate their cars and trucks for the parade . . . We want to drive away the depression blues of 1932 and greet 1933 with bright hopes and smiles.''

(From the *Tribune*, December 31st, 1932.)

That this parade was organised by the Lodges is significant. In describing the roots of the mass political movement of the 1950s and 1960s, Dame Doris Johnson pointed out a link between organised labour and the Lodges. ''The years from 1931 to 1936,'' she writes,

saw the country plunged into economic depression which plummeted the resources to a new low . . .

The plight of the labouring man now came to the notice of the brothers in the lodges. The time had come, they felt, to organise the masses — if their lot was to improve . . . Charles Rhoderiquez [a prominent member of the Elks Lodge] led the organisation of the first labour union in 1935, and in 1936 the Labour Minimum Wage Act was passed. By 1942, the sleeping giant was beginning to rouse.

(From *The Quiet Revolution in The Bahamas,*
1972.)

Bahamians had not been immune to the trends of the age. During the early 1930s, various unions and cooperatives had sprung up throughout the colony. Most significant of these were the Bahamas Labour Union, established in 1936, whose membership consisted largely of unskilled workers, and the Bahamas Federation of Labour, made up of artisans and skilled labourers. Disorganised protest was not uncommon; the newspapers reported labour unrest in both Nassau and Inagua as early as 1935, the first year of the West Indian strikes, and this unrest would continue throughout the decade, providing fertile ground for a disturbance in Matthew Town in 1937, and a political protest in Nassau in 1938. There was, however, no one body which could speak for the mass of workers. Thus, although there were isolated incidents of labour unrest throughout The Bahamas, none was cohesive enough to bring pressure to bear on the upper classes.

It is significant, however, that in Junkanoo, the Bahamian workers were still able to parade as one. Not that the parades were totally unified — neighbourhood groups once more banded together against men from other districts, and fighting was common. The same argument, however, may be advanced for labour-inspired riots elsewhere in the Caribbean. What is notable about the Junkanoo parades on Bay Street was that, once there, the fighting took on a game-like, almost symbolic quality.

In his dissertation, Dr Keith Wisdom argues:

Junkanoo Ribbons (National Gallery of Jamaica)

Junkanoo seems to have been a unifying element within [the black Bahamian community] since at least the early nineteenth century . . .

Junkanoo, in uniting ordinarily disparate elements of the community in a single event . . . has ignored hierarchical elements in the Bahamas [thus] irritat[ing] middle class Black Bahamians as well as the White colonial and neo-colonial power structure.

(From Keith Wisdom, *Bahamian Junkanoo: An Act in a Modern Social Drama*, 1985.)

The significance of Junkanoo's role during the restless 1930s grows when we consider Dr Saunders' comment that "during the summer when jobs were scarce, and the climate oppressive, . . . most incidents of unrest occurred" (*Social History*, 1985.); what she has not added is the fact that, during the winter months, in addition to having employment, the workers also took part in Junkanoo. And for a time, perhaps, participation was enough. Perhaps the mere symbolism of the parades — a mass occupation of Bay Street for a night — was sufficient to appease the labouring classes and keep them from protesting more violently.

It is possible that when the masqueraders appeared without costumes something more than their poverty was being expressed. Perhaps the labourers, fully aware of the ruling classes' interest in Junkanoo purely as a tourist spectacle, had decided, consciously or not, to deny them that spectacle. The idea is not so terribly far-fetched when we remember the masqueraders' decision in 1923 not to give the Bay Street merchants their business on Christmas morning; black Bahamians were fully aware of the power of Junkanoo. It is possible, therefore, to read in the roughness of the parades the labourers' protest against their conditions — in the only way legally available to them.

It can thus be argued that, owing in part to these annual

street demonstrations, the Bahamian workers were able to postpone the riot which would link them to their West Indian brothers. But the riot was only postponed for a time. Junkanoo, although a vehicle for social comment, was by itself not a vehicle for social change. Riot, which had worked for the West Indian masses, was inevitable in Nassau.

The Burma Road Riots occurred in the colony in the summer of 1942. They are said to have been started by an unresolved wage dispute. When Bahamian workers employed on the construction of the proposed American Air Force bases in New Providence discovered that they were being paid considerably less than their American counterparts, they stormed Bay Street, smashing windows and looting shops. The true roots of the disturbance, however, lay in the events of the whole post-Prohibition era.

The Air Force bases in question were a joint War project of the English-speaking Allies. Concerned about the threat of Nazi submarine activity in the Caribbean, the United States had agreed with Great Britain to establish an Operational Training Unit in New Providence. Under the agreement, and for reasons never made clear, Bahamian labour was to be hired at local wages.

Two areas of New Providence were chosen as sites for the bases. The first site, an extension of the existing Oakes Field, would be the Main Field, and was located just south of Grant's Town. The second, called Satellite Field, was situated in the Pine Barrens near the western end of the island; the road between the two was known as Burma Road. An American company, Pleasantville Incorporated, was engaged to construct the air bases, and building began on May 20th, 1942.

At first the 'Project' — as the two sites came to be known — was seen as a blessing by the many unemployed labourers in the city. The entry of the United States into the War the previous winter had brought tourism to a halt, and had threatened to return the colony to the poverty of the pre-Oakes years; the Project was offering as many as 2,000 jobs. What was more, the prospect of working for Americans was appealing to those people who had experienced American wages elsewhere. It was a shock to the Bahamians employed on the Project, then, to discover that they were to be paid four shillings a day — no more than they had received on other construction sites. What was more, the Pleasantville Company had brought in a substantial number of white Americans, who were being paid at American rates; and a rumour was being circulated that the company had been prepared to pay the Bahamians equally well, but was prevented from doing so by the colony's government.

The workers, dissatisfied, appealed to Charles Rhoderiquez, then leader of both the Labour Union and the Federation of Labour, for help. A meeting was held, the problem discussed, and a letter dispatched to the Labour Officer proposing an adjusted scale of payment. The reply came that, as the House of Assembly had been dissolved in preparation for general elections in June, and the Duke of Windsor (who was Governor at the time) was away, the situation could not immediately be resolved. Rhoderiquez informed the workers, and the matter was considered settled. The workers, however, were not satisfied. On Sunday May 31st, a number of them took their case to the Pleasantville office at Main Field; their case heard, they were dispersed by police officers wielding sticks. The next day, armed with sticks and cutlasses, the labourers assembled once more at Main Field, and, refusing to work, began to march into town to take their grievances to the Colonial Secretary. As they marched, they sang. When they reached Bay Street, they were at first quiet, waiting for the response from the Colonial Secretary; once more, nothing concrete was offered. Then, their options exhausted, the crowd became violent, breaking windows and looting the shops on Bay Street.

The police force and a detachment of Cameron Highlanders, garrisoned in Nassau since the establishment of the Project, drove the rioters Over-the-Hill, where the violence continued until the Duke's return the next day. In all, extensive damage was done to property, five lives were lost, and many people injured.

The government and the newly-appointed labour leaders were staggered. Such behaviour was considered entirely out of keeping with the Bahamian character. To appease the workers, therefore, the Duke arranged for a one-shilling pay rise, plus a hot meal each day on site — little enough, for the same labour conditions had been offered by Harry Oakes eight years earlier. The resolution, however, was accepted by both sides, and by June 8th, work resumed on the Project.

At first glance, the events of June 1942 had little to do with Junkanoo. Several factors about the riots, however, associate them with the festival. First, the fact that the workers planned the march into town and then sang as they went suggests that they were accompanied also by drummers. Traditionally, all such deputations — the nineteenth-century marches to Government House, the Elks' parade of the early thirties, and even protest marches of more recent years — were held to the beat of goombay drums. Second, as Dr Keith Wisdom has pointed out, the temporary occupation of Bay Street was a custom popularised by the junkanoos; during the 1942 riots, that symbolic occupation was carried to its violent extreme. And finally, like the disturbances at the site of the Hotel Colonial twenty years earlier, Burma Road inspired a junkanoo song that is still sung today. The lyrics of "Goin' Down Burma Road" not only tell the real story of the riots, but re-create the rhythm of the march:

Burma Road declare war on da Conchy Joe,
Do nigger, don't lick nobody.

By 1942, then, The Bahamas had had its riot. Unlike the other West Indian colonies, however, there was no immediate difference in the system of government after the disturbance. The tradition of limited representative rule, entrenched since 1729, left little room for real social change; what it did do was curb the power of both the Governor and the people, and concentrate it in the hands of the white mercantile elite. Life for the workers after the riots, with some exceptions, was essentially the same as it had been before.

Nor were the exceptions, on the whole, positive. The government, badly shaken, took precautions against any similar disturbance breaking out in the future, and banned all public gatherings. This ruling, as a matter of course, included the Junkanoo parades, but in 1944, a special prohibition was placed on the festival. Junkanoo had become far more than the mere "street nuisance" that the 1899 Act had made it; it was now specifically illegal.

But a custom so embedded in the psyche of a people dies hard, and although the junkanoos were not seen on Bay Street for many years, the following newspaper reports attest to the fact that they were very active elsewhere on the island.

Unlawful Parade

During the early part of last evening a hundred or more people paraded through several streets in the Southern District, ringing cow bells and beating drums, in spite of the fact that an order under the Defence Act Regulations strictly forbids these parades. The police are undoubtedly taking steps to prevent this breach of the law.

(From the *Nassau Guardian*, December 22, 1942.)

Illegal Parade

A fairly large 'John Canoe' parade was seen last night in the neighbourhood of Oakes Field in spite of the present regulations forbidding such gatherings. Many of the men taking part in the Parade carried large sticks with which they tapped passing cars, though no damage was done. The incident was reported to the Police and we trust that every precaution is being taken to enforce the regulations in this respect.

(From the *Nassau Guardian*, December 24, 1943.)

New Year's Eve Parade Dispersed

During New Year's Eve and New Year's morning the Police were obliged to disperse several crowds of men who were parading through some streets ringing cowbells and making other noises. Several men were arrested and convicted in the Magistrate's Court this morning on charges of disturbing the peace.

(From the *Nassau Guardian*, January 3, 1944.)

This unhealthy state of affairs continued until the end of the war, after which new sources of income needed to be found. Once more, the government turned to tourism and real estate, and new, far more aggressive policies for their devleopment were established. Partly as a result of repeated petitions on the part of the Junkanoo Committee, but largely because the government saw in Junkanoo a powerful tourist attraction, the parades were again officially recognised in 1947.

The *Guardian*'s comment was dubious:

A Committee, recently formed, has raised by public subscription money enough to provide valuable cash prizes for the best costumes, and this incentive will no doubt provoke competitive efforts to restore some of the glories of carnival times of former years. But this in itself is not enough. It will be remembered that it was the gradual degeneration of our annual John Canoe Parade into a mere pretext for hooliganism that eventually led to their disappearance. It is by their conduct — perhaps more than by their costumes — that the public will judge the masqueraders this New Year. Seemly behaviour is by no means incompatible with the carnival spirit; jollity need not reduce riotousness or intemperance, but these former rather banish the latter. It would be well if these considerations were taken into account in the awarding of the prizes. The John Canoes are being weighed in the balance; and it rests entirely with them not to be found wanting. The police will be expected to exercise great vigilance.

(From the *Nassau Guardian*, December 29, 1947.)

But on January 1st, 1948, triumphantly, Junkanoo took place on Bay Street.

Celebrating (private collection)

7
Law, Order and Discipline

Junkanoo in The Bahamas: 1948 – 1990

Reorganisation 1948 – 1960

The return of Junkanoo to Bay Street was greeted by enthusiastic crowds. "Onto the narrow . . . sidewalks, designed to hold only a few hundred, . . . parades were now drawing as many as 5,000 people," writes Dr Keith Wisdom. (From *Bahamian Junkanoo; An Act in a Modern Social Drama,* 1985.). In the early years of its reinstatement, however, the number of non-costumed 'rushers' far exceeded the number of those in disguise. As a result, the role of the Citizen's Masquerade Committee (as it was now called) became more prominent, and a massive reordering of the festival was deemed necessary. What was wanted once more was a spectacle for tourists. No longer, therefore, could the masqueraders be permitted to 'rush' any way they chose; rules were imposed and the parade civilised.

The reorganisation of Junkanoo took two forms. One was external: the parade grew in rigidity of structure as guidelines were imposed by the Masquerade Committee and enforced by the government and the police. The other was internal and spontaneous, carried out by the participants themselves.

The earliest evidence of internal organisation occurred during the early 1950s. In 1954, for instance, the first Junkanoo band to wear matching costumes appeared. Led by three entertainers — David Kemp, Maureen Duvalier and Bruce

Beneby — they entered as 'the Mexicans', and proceeded not only to march down Bay Street, but also to perform. The Mexicans consisted of eighteen dancers and fifteen musicians; the dancers wore black satin, and their accompanists, five drummers and ten cowbellers, costumes of red, white and black paper fringe. The idea was quick to catch on. By 1956, several other groups had adopted matching fringed costumes; and by 1958, the practice had become refined enough for various groups to use different combinations of colours as identification.

By the middle of the decade, too, the idea of performing for the crowd had also become popular. In the small hours of Boxing and New Year's Days, various night-club entertainers made a habit of heading, complete with entourage, directly from their shows to Bay Street, and the tradition of 'rushing' was complemented by the new custom of dancing for the crowd. Among them were people who would eventually become Junkanoo legends: 'Sweet Richard' Dean, the Kemp brothers, David and Johnny, Maureen Duvalier and the Chipman family.

Much of the cause for Junkanoo's growing popularity undoubtedly lay in the prosperity which followed the Second World War. Tourism and foreign investment were, as already mentioned, its joint foundation. Once again The Bahamas was profiting from the well-being of its largest neighbour; thus, as the post-war years were boom times for the United States, they were similarly comfortable in Nassau. Again, the Bahamian government was quick to exploit the ease with which one could invest money in the colony, and consequently much revenue was accumulated.

Tourism was the source of a good deal of new wealth for whites and blacks alike. Improved transportation and the new tendency for the ordinary American to travel brought many visitors to the colony. What was more, the face of the industry was changing. In 1949, the Development Board had come under the direction of Stafford Sands, a white lawyer and businessman and the possessor of one of the most ruthless, brilliant minds in the colony. Sands capitalised on the legacies of the War years — the two new airports and, morbidly, the international notoriety brought to Nassau by the 1943 murder of Sir Harry Oakes — and, employing aggressive American-style advertising techniques, he had begun to promote the colony abroad. His tactics turned profits. "By the beginning . . . of the 1950s, The Bahamas was attracting not only the wealthy, titled, and famous, but those in the middle income bracket as well." (Gail Saunders, *The Social History of The Bahamas, 1890-1953*, 1985.)

Junkanoo, of course, was one of the attractions, and was promoted as aggressively as any other. With it, Sands took few chances. Like Harold Christie before him, he recognised the appeal of Junkanoo's carnival aspect, and set about encouraging its development. In the early fifties, for instance, he sent a delegation of Bahamian entertainers to Florida to observe parades there. Among them were David Kemp and Maureen Duvalier, two of the founders of the Mexicans, and pioneers of the organised Junkanoo group. (Keith Wisdom, interview, 30 August, 1990.)

In response to the increasing demand for an orderly Junkanoo celebration, the Masquerade Committee boosted the awards. Not only were prizes given to the best individual costumes; now groups were also encouraged to organise themselves, and the most attractive rewarded. As a result, several entrants began to spend more time on the construction and design of their costumes. This fresh approach to the parade attracted a new set of rushers:

> Junkanoo began to gain acceptance and respectability, via the art of costume design, with middle class Blacks who not only began to participate in 'Over-the-hill' organised Junkanoo groups, but also learned and developed the crafts of Junkanoo and began to organise their own neighbourhood groups.
> (From Keith Wisdom, *Bahamian Junkanoo: An Act in a Modern Social Drama*, 1985.)

Economic prosperity was not the only cause of the new acceptability of the Junkanoo parade. The decades following the War brought social and political changes as well as economic growth. The years of struggling to provide black children with sound educations were coming to fruition, and the late 1940s and early 1950s saw the return of the first group of young black professionals to the colony. Educated at Government High and finished in England, most of them were lawyers, and all of them had been infected with the nationalist fever then sweeping the colonial students in London. These men came home to set up their own law practices, thus giving the black majority access to fair legal representation for the first time. They also carried their quest for equality into the political arena; a decade and a half later, many of them would form the first black Bahamian government.

Educational improvements were to affect the course of Junkanoo in unexpected ways. By the 1950s, in addition to Government High, there existed various private high schools which admitted black students. In 1945, Benedictine monks had opened St Augustine's College for boys, the first private high school with no colour barrier. Two years later, the

Anglican church established St John's College. Although created primarily for young men wishing to enter the priesthood, St John's became a popular high school among Anglican families, and many children were educated there; and as the vast majority of Anglicans in The Bahamas were black, the College became one of the pioneers in the private education of coloured Bahamians. Even Queen's College, whose admission had for so long been restricted to whites, was forced by the Methodist Missionary Society in London to open its doors. The black community, no longer dependent solely upon the Government High School for the secondary education of its youngsters, embarked on a path of upward mobility which would transform the face of Junkanoo. It is no accident that the high school athletes who founded the Valley Boys in the late 1950s were students of St John's College; the impact that group would have on the future development of Junkanoo would underscore the contribution made by the growing black middle classes to the parade.

The era also brought with it a fresh spate of social and intellectual activity among black Bahamians. Strengthened by the riots, for example, the trade unions found at last a solid foundation among the masses. The changing economy also provided them with additional power. No longer were the Bahamian workers scattered, employed in many different jobs and working in various corners of the archipelago; the development of tourism and investment had set the centre of employment squarely in the capital. Bahamians were now overwhelmingly engaged in the tourist trade. Membership in the relevant unions grew, and the power of the labour leaders grew with it.

What was more, the majority had finally found a voice for itself. Unhappy with the daily newspapers as a medium for their views, coloured Bahamians created their own periodicals. Of these, the most significant was undoubtedly *The Nassau*

Earth and Sea Fantasy (Shell Bahamas Ltd)

Herald, a biweekly publication which was critical of the status quo. Less radical was the *Bahamian Review Magazine,* whose edge was blunted by the fact that it relied upon the *Guardian*'s presses for its existence. However, its editors — William Cartwright and Cyril Stevenson — were not inactive in the fight for equality. As their concern with the colony's social climate grew, so did their involvement in politics. In time, they were joined by Henry Taylor, an educator and thinker, and in 1953, realising that the most effective way to combat the political monopoly of the white merchants was to form a single organisation behind which all other Bahamians could unite, these men established the Progressive Liberal Party. It was with this group that the returning lawyers aligned themselves; and foremost among them was the young Lynden Pindling, who joined upon his return from university in October 1953.

The formation of the P.L.P. was the first independent action taken by the majority of Bahamians. The ruling minority had no choice but to respond, and for a time, Bahamian politics were marked by further offensive actions taken by blacks, followed by the government's reactions to those moves. In 1956, for instance, the government voted for the ending of legal segregation in the colony; and in 1958, the members of the white oligarchy created the United Bahamian Party. It is possible to view the formation of the U.B.P. as the first real political victory gained by blacks in The Bahamas, for it marked the start of an era of rapid political reform.

In 1958, too, the new strength of the unions was made evident by the success of a general strike. The previous year had seen the entry of the labour movement into the political struggle when another lawyer, Randol Fawkes, had established the Bahamas Federation of Labour. In January 1958, certain white merchants formed a tour car company to transport visitors from the new airport at Windsor Field to the hotels.

Angered by this move, the Taxicab Union organised a blockade of the airport roads. Both the B.F.L. and the P.L.P. supported this action, instituting a sympathy strike by all Bahamian labourers. The strike lasted for nineteen days, at the end of which the tour car monopoly was removed — another victory for the black majority. It is possible, then, to view the 1950s as a decade in which black Bahamians were beginning to sense their united power.

As the black population became more conscious of its power in society, its activity in Junkanoo was transformed. In contrast to the parades of the thirties, which reflected closely the hardship of the times, those of the fifties provided entertainment, an escape from daily concerns, rather than a rallying-point for those who wished to protest. It is true that the parade became more sophisticated; the costumes carried by individuals illustrate this. Gone were the horses' heads and cows' horns of earlier decades. In their place were costumes whose designs reflected the new Nassau — cruise ships, aeroplanes and the like. Disappearing too were disguises made of 'junk'; the festival had its status symbols, as did life, and costumes made from sponge, leaves, bottle caps and other scraps were abandoned in favour of those created from cloth and fringed tissue paper. Even more significant was the absence, in these parades, of the traditional Junkanoo songs. No longer did the masqueraders create satirical social commentaries, like those of the early decades of the century, to sing on Boxing Day and New Year's mornings. Instead, they provided entertainment for the crowds which turned out to see them.

It seemed at times, indeed, as though the job of the Masquerade Committee was being preempted by the actions of the paraders themselves. It was the junkanoos of the era who were primarily responsible for the transformation of the festival. Junkanoo was becoming more and more attractive to watch, as was demonstrated by the growing number of spectators who gathered on Bay Street each year; it was changing, in fact, from a festival in which all were free to take part into a folklore show put on by performers for an audience.

By the end of the fifties, then, Junkanoo had lost some of its roughness, and had taken on several of the characteristics of the modern parade. It is significant, for instance, that the parade was no longer referred to as the 'Masquerade' or the 'Johnny Canoes', but had become known to all by the name it would hold in years to come, as if at last all Bahamians were beginning to recognise the festival as something truly their own. It was the next decade, however, which would see the emergence of a truly modern celebration.

Consolidation 1960 – 1973

In his dissertation on Junkanoo, Keith Wisdom comments:

between 1953 and 1973, in terms of the development of Bahamian party politics, a major political struggle or 'social drama' occurred. The culmination of this social drama was political independence and black rule. It is within the process of this drama that modern Bahamian Junkanoo can best be understood.

(From *Bahamian Junkanoo: An Act in a Modern Social Drama*, 1985.)

A quick survey of the political changes occurring in the 1960s and early 1970s bears him out: in 1960, the U.B.P., still shaken by the success of the general strike, agreed to certain electoral reforms, the most significant of which was the granting of the vote to women. It is likely that this move was not completely selfless on the part of the ruling party; women were considered to be more conservative than men, and the

U.B.P. politicians hoped that the female vote would help return them to the House of Assembly in the next general election. When the results of the 1962 elections were tallied, moreover, their hopes seemed fulfilled; once again, the U.B.P. had won by a landslide. It is simplistic, however, to say that Bahamian women were responsible for putting the white merchants back into power. It is far more likely that the U.B.P. majority in the house was maintained largely by gerrymandering, for while the white merchants had gained more seats than before, the P.L.P. had received the bulk of the votes.

In 1964, the colony received a new constitution, extending its right to self-government; the first premier, Roland Symonette, was apppointed, and a U.B.P. cabinet formed. The power of the white merchants, it seemed, had never been greater. Three years later, however, that power was proved illusory; the 1967 general elections saw the P.L.P. win an equal number of seats as the government. Once again, success was achieved by the uniting of the P.L.P. with the representatives of labour. The tie was broken when Randol Fawkes, the sole representative of the B.F.L. in the House, joined the P.L.P. to become the first black Minister of Labour. In 1968 a second election gave an overwhelming majority of the seats in the House to the P.L.P.; thus the era of white rule in The Bahamas was ended.

Unlike their counterparts in the 1930s, the junkanoos did not play an active role in these changes. In the first place, the sharp identification between the working man and Junkanoo had been blurred by the entry into the parade of representatives of the educated middle class, who were bent on the continued development of the art of Junkanoo. In the second place, the shape of protest had changed. No longer did it stem from the working class *en masse*, as it had done even as late as the fifties; now, all such protest was led by various members of the political parties, most of them professional men. More

The actions of the Masquerade Committee helped solidify this change. During the 1960s and early 1970s, its members took radical steps to secure a tighter organisation of the parade, and many new regulations were imposed. First, as a measure of protection for the costumes, no one without a disguise was allowed on the streets during the parades; and in 1966, in order to ensure that this ruling was followed, metal barricades were placed along the sides of the street and the parade route was cordoned off. This tended to isolate the costumed paraders and also to accentuate the gap between performer and audience. In addition, it was decided that, in order to preserve a craft that seemed uniquely Bahamian, only those costumes entirely made of paper fringe would be eligible for awards, thus effectively curbing the tradition of creating art from 'junk'.

As time passed, this combination of regulation and reward succeeded in creating two main types of junkanoo participants. First, as the more orderly atmosphere of the parade occasioned the growth of the art of Junkanoo, new groups were formed, each more innovative than the last, and each vying for the prestige — and the money — which came from winning one of the parades. The 'Valley Boys' began that refinement of organised participation which would make them one of the greatest competitors in the history of modern Junkanoo. Having adopted, like other groups, the custom of using colour to unify, they began to perfect it. In 1960, entering as Scottish Highlanders, they abandoned the traditional shirt-and-trouser costume, instead introducing shoulder-pieces and skirts which were, like the headpieces, made of cardboard and fringed. These pieces moved as the junkanoos themselves moved, thus complementing the rhythm of the drums. The Valley Boys also revolutionised group marching, organising their members in lines and having the group leaders go before them, performing for the crowd. The overall effect was almost military, and was

Head-dress (Mr E. Moseley, Nassau)

and more of those who 'rushed', therefore, did so for personal creative fulfillment, and not as an expression of solidarity, and Junkanoo was transformed as a result.

immediately adopted by other groups.

Theme and costume were quick to replace the performances which had characterised the 1950s, and individual competitors were overshadowed by the visual impact of the groups. In 1963, a new band entered the parade, and its theme, 'Saxons', secured its name. Although many of its members were still young, it would soon prove itself worthy of competing with the established groups, and the competition it offered helped accelerate the development which marked this era. Two years later, the 'Vikings', a group which had been performing for the last decade, won first prize by bringing to Bay Street card-board sculptures representing their theme. Their 'living hibiscus' were in effect giant flowers made of cardboard, wood and wire, which enclosed the men who carried them. In 1966, the 'Vikings' further refined their art by using wire from chicken coops to create wings which moved, thus carrying the idea of dynamic costumes a step beyond the 'Valley Boys'. Rivalry among the groups was so fierce, however, that one year's victor was often defeated the next; by 1967, the 'Valley Boys' were building similar costumes, and winning. They were followed closely by the 'Saxons', whose victory on New Year's Day 1969 earned them a place in 'respectable' Junkanoo. By the end of the decade, therefore, the festival seemed to have been taken over by the organised groups.

While the new custom of parading for prizes made Junkanoo a spectacle which attracted increasing numbers of watchers each year, the tradition of rushing for fun was slow to die. While the rivalry for supremacy in costume design and group organisation raged among the new-style junkanoos, another competition was taking place: those participants who continued with pride the age-old practice of marching down Bay Street for no other reward than the thrill of it were pitting themselves against the large groups. Their costumes were crude, their groups poorly organised and their manner rowdy;

their main purpose was to make music and enjoy themselves, and, because they still made costumes from any material they could find, they were quickly given the name of 'scrappers'. Throughout the 1960s, the membership of scrap gangs remained high.

It was possible for a spectator at a parade of the time to witness the literal meeting of two eras of Junkanoo. It is also possible for us now, looking back, to see in the scrappers and groupers on Bay Street the meeting of two branches of Bahamian history. The scrap gangs, which still 'rushed' in celebration of a temporary freedom, may be seen as repre-senting the black Nassauvians of the early twentieth century, who found in Junkanoo an outlet for their woes. The big groups, on the other hand, which had, in concert with the Masquerade Committee, imposed an order on Junkanoo which was new to the parade, might stand for the second half of the century, when black Bahamians began to rule themselves. The theory is further strengthened by the virtual dying out of scrap participation in the parades of the 1990s; in a society where the dream of becoming middle class still seems attainable, there is no apparent need for working-class solidarity.

For the Bahamians in post-war Nassau, however, if their involvement in Junkanoo was in any way political, it was unconsciously so. Keith Wisdom states as much:

> The Junkanoo parades of the 1950s, 1960s and early 1970s were not symbolic representations of the desire for socio-political transformations in The Bahamas . . . so much as iconic, direct embodiments of these same desires.

(From *Bahamian Junkanoo: An Act in a Modern Social Drama*, 1985.)

Sky warrior (private collection)

There is more to it than that. The 1960s brought with them not only a change in government for the Bahamian people; they brought too an adjustment in attitudes. The victory of the P.L.P. in 1967 sparked, for the blacks, both an interest in the African heritage which had long been suppressed and a desire to attain the economic and social standing so long denied them by the whites. For Bahamians of the 1970s, Junkanoo would come to represent the very core of their culture, present and past. After Independence, Junkanoo would move from the realm of spontaneous celebration to that of stylised representation, and in so doing would lose some of its links with tradition. At the same time, however, it would become the subject of much debate and study; it would thus provide Bahamians with a channel by which to explore their heritage.

Contemporary 1973 – 1990

Junkanoo of the early 1970s was a far cry from the festival of a decade or so earlier. With majority rule and independence had come a greater sense of self-confidence among blacks, and practices which expressed their African heritage were given prominence in the new society. Junkanoo was declared a 'national treasure', and its development promoted by the new government. At the same time, encouraged perhaps by the Black Pride movement in the United States, individual Bahamians began to recognise the parade's value, and the necessity of developing it as a unique art form was publicised. Workshops were held on the art of drumming, belling and costume-making; the junkanoo beat was adopted by popular musicians as the rhythm underlying their work, and traditional junkanoo songs were recorded and released; choreographers studied Junkanoo dance steps and placed them, stylised, on

stage; Bahamian artists, inspired by the colour and life of the parade, began creating paintings and sculptures which used the festival as their subject; writers and scholars took Junkanoo for their themes, attempting to capture it in verse, or to discover its origins in their theses. Not unnaturally, the festival changed, growing bigger and more popular with the years.

The transformation of Junkanoo was not all the result of social factors. As Keith Wisdom notes: "1966 marked the beginning of a wave of rules and regulations which effected an 'ordering' of Bahamian Junkanoo that helped define [modern] Junkanoo." (From *Bahamian Junkanoo: An Act in a Modern Social Drama*, 1985.) The Masquerade Committee became the Junkanoo Committee, and, assisted by the Ministry of Tourism, created new rules and offered attractive awards; first prize for groups during this period was increased to $1,000. These intensified the entrants' compptititive spirit, and Junkanoo became as much a contest as it was a show.

As the art of creating junkanoo costumes developed, too, the expense of participating in the parade increased, and the largest groups sought sponsorship from various businesses to help them cover their costs. The festival became a form of advertisement for these businesses, and the stakes in the competition were again raised; as a result, the big groups flourished, and individual competitors were slowly forced into positions of less prominence in the parade.

Themes, too, were different from those of previous years. In the 1950s, when most costumes were the work of individuals, they had often depicted some part of the new economy; the growth of group competition in the 1960s brought with it the development of martial themes — Scottish Highlanders, Vikings and Saxons — whose roots were essentially foreign, usually European. Of the 1970s, however, Keith Wisdom notes that "most of the artistic representations . . . took as their focus the natural beauty of The Bahamas, for example, the

Goblins from Afar (Shell Bahamas Ltd)

island geography, wild life and indigenous flora.'' (From *Bahamian Junkanoo: An Act in a Modern Social Drama*, 1985.) Other, more racially-conscious motifs also emerged: themes included tributes to African monarchs, celebrations of ancient civilisations (Egypt, India and China) and representations of various pre-Columbian American cultures.

Groups grew in size, and with them the costumes also grew, until they assumed gigantic proportions. Parades of the 1970s saw whole floats covered in fringed crepe paper make their appearance on Junkanoo mornings; on those floats would be huge tableaux depicting the group's theme, and these would be pushed or pulled along the route by men, also covered in coloured fringe, and surrounded by musicians.

A contemporary description might serve to illustrate the changed face of Junkanoo. In 1977, my father wrote in his dissertation:

The Junkanoos ... have become better organised. Today fewer individual entrants are seen as they are gradually being replaced by large groups. Numbering between 40 and 200, these bands are sponsored by local business houses, which finance the now expensive construction of the costumes. Striving for originality, each group selects a theme, which is carried out in every detail by all members of the group.

Designing and constructing the costumes begin months before Christmas. Large sheds are used for this purpose as the costumes are made in secrecy so that rival groups do not see each other's designs until the day of the Festival itself. The technique of applying the paper fringe to the under garment of the costume has become more and more refined, and the former coarse fringing has given way to a fringe so fine that it resembles shredded coconut.

Each group provides its own music. The musicians, who formerly had clustered around the principal drummers in 'gangs', are now strung out in long lines so that all members of the group can hear the rhythms. In some cases when the band is especially large, more than one group of musicians is required.

The costumes have become so enormous, in some cases cumbersome and unwieldy, that a height restriction of 11 ft had to be imposed. In addition, because of the huge size, two-way Junkanoo traffic on Bay Street became virtually impossible. As a result, a circular one-way route utilising more streets was introduced in 1973. While it must be admitted that the new arrangement makes for a smoother flow of traffic, one no longer hears the interesting clash of contrasting rhythms which used to occur when one band passed another going in the opposite direction.

Another feature of the 1970s was the reintroduction of melody into the festival. By the time the parade had been reinstated in 1947, the songs which had accompanied the rushers had disappeared. For the thirty-odd years which followed Junkanoo was performed to the rhythmic, tuneless music of horns and bells, with occasional random bugle-notes adding variety to the beat. In 1976, however, a new junkanoo group appeared, featuring not only a fresh approach to costume-making and theme, but also a brass section among its musicians, which played traditional junkanoo tunes as the band 'rushed'. The 'Music Makers', as the group was called, won the parades of that season and the next, and for the better part of the next decade provided the impetus for a new leg of development in Junkanoo.

The new trends were not popular with all, however, as my father noted:

To many an old-timer, who remembers the spontaneity and sheer fun of the pre-'60s parades, the Festival has now become too organised. They claim that the Festival has now become nothing more than a parade of costumes. Furthermore, they contend that even these costumes, brilliant though they might be, have lost the essential element of the old masquerade parades, for today masks are no longer required.

All these points may be valid, but the spirit of Junkanoo is not entirely lost. Every Boxing Day and New Year's Day, there are still those who cannot control the irresistible urge to 'rush'. In order to qualify as 'costumed' Junkanoos, they attach the barest minimum of paper fringe to their everyday clothes, take out their cowbells, drums and whistles and join the parade. These 'scrap gangs', as they are called, add much to the spirit of the occasion, (and, in many cases, the best music), and the fact that they are often composed of youngsters augers well for the further development of the Festival.

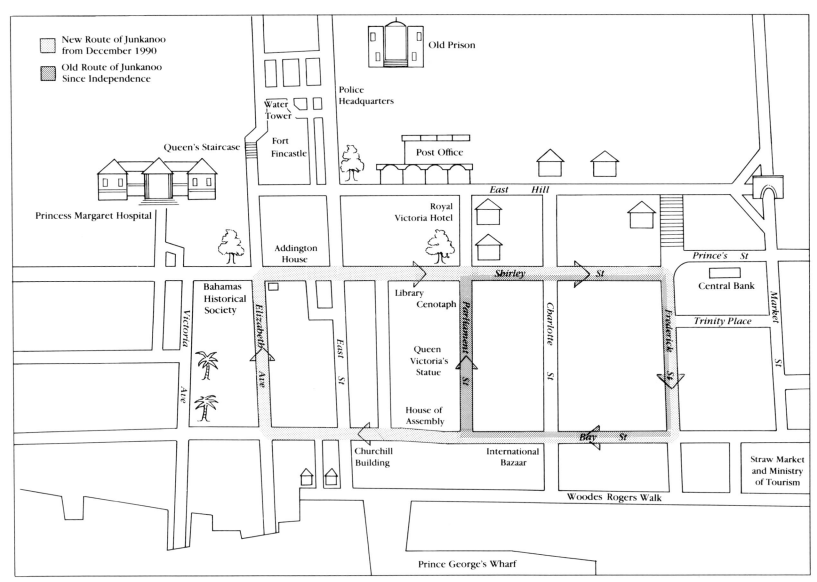

New Route of Junkanoo from December 1990

Old Route of Junkanoo Since Independence

Old Prison

Police Headquarters

Water Tower

Fort Fincastle

Queen's Staircase

Post Office

Princess Margaret Hospital

East   Hill

Royal Victoria Hotel

Prince's   St

Addington House

Central Bank

Bahamas Historical Society

Shirley   *St*

Library Cenotaph

Parliament St

Charlotte St

Frederick St

Trinity Place

Victoria Ave

Elizabeth Ave

East St

Queen Victoria's Statue

Market St

House of Assembly

Churchill Building

International Bazaar

Bay   St

Straw Market and Ministry of Tourism

Woodes Rogers Walk

Prince George's Wharf

Modern Junkanoo Route

By the start of the 1980s, however, despite his optimistic observation about 'scrap', the festival was dominated by a triumvirate of 'super-groups' which had grown up during the 1970s, and was ceasing to be a people's celebration. These groups — The 'Music Makers', the 'Saxons Superstars', and the 'Valley Boys' — were largely responsible for the current sophistication of the parade, and the latter two would continue to inspire new development during the next decade. The division between 'groupers' and 'scrappers' had now grown so deep that it bordered on hostility. As the presentation of themes continued to increase in complexity and beauty, order was crucial to the development of the large groups' art. It was also necessary to the survival of the groups themselves, for in return for corporate sponsorship, one was expected to win on Bay Street. The continued existence of scrap gangs in the parade was considered a hindrance to such victory; scrappers, traditionally opposed to organisation, often impeded the performance of the groups.

The Junkanoo Committee, too, opposed the participation of scrap gangs in the parade. It was now in a better position to institute its rulings. In 1982, it had been transferred from the Ministry of Tourism to the Ministry of Youth, and thus came under a staff dedicated to the development of culture not for visitors, but for its own sake. Faced with a parade which combined the groups' strict organisation with the wildness which characterised spectators and scrap, the committee took as its focus the maintenance of crowd control. Scrap groups were perceived as unruly, and their hastily-made costumes made them the perfect camouflage for members of the public who wanted unauthorised access to the street; the crowd was disorderly and posed a danger to the big groups' costumes. To offset these problems, bleachers (tiered benches) were set up along Bay Street, and places on them sold. At the same time, rules were drawn up governing appearance and conduct in the parade. All prospective junkanoos had to register either as groups or as individuals, and had to state a theme; the registration forms provided access onto the route. The regulation of the Junkanoo participants, it was hoped, would thus provide a suitable atmosphere for the continued development of the art.

Such restrictions ran counter to the philosophy of the scappers. "Scrap," in the words of Dr Wisdom,

> refers to a group or an individual who spends very little time in preparation of his Junkanoo costume and participates in Junkanoo because of the unstructured freedom the event allows the individual performer.
>
> (From *Bahamian Junkanoo: An Act in a Modern Social Drama*, 1985.)

To be a scrapper during the eighties, therefore, was no longer terribly rewarding. One could neither hope to win a prize, nor to have a satisfying 'rush'; and as the size of groups grew, congestion on the route became worse and worse, and freedom of movement was difficult. Perhaps even more discouraging for scappers was the fact that the spectators had come out to see costumes, and to support one or the other of the big groups, and any other entrant was unlikely to be well-received. Many scrap gangs disbanded as a result, and their members drifted into the ranks of the major competitors. However, as one former scrapper put it, "it ain't the same." (Interview with Charles 'Fuzzie' Moss Jr., November 19th, 1987.)

The new regulations, while cleaning up the route and strengthening the existing super-groups, also created a climate which made it difficult for smaller organised groups to flourish. The growth of the major competitors which occurred with the decline of scrap resulted in monster groups comprising anywhere from three to five hundred members, all sporting costumes of one sort or another; this in turn worsened the congestion on the route, and slowed the 'rush' of Junkanoo to a crawl. The cost of competing with the major groups was also prohibitive. As the decade progressed, the expense of mounting a parade increased, and financial difficulties resulted in the failure of numerous smaller groups. Ten years earlier, sponsors had not found it very difficult to meet the expense of mounting a parade. By the late eighties, however, when the average cost of taking a group to Bay Street had increased to roughly $30,000 (from the National Junkanoo Committee's ''Report on First National Conference on Junkanoo'', March 1988), Junkanoo demanded a level of monetary support which few enterprises could offer. Consequently, many small groups sank into oblivion after just two or three years of participation. Juvenile junkanoo bands, an important source of creative talent during the 1950s and 1960s, vanished almost altogether as the super-groups opened their ranks to children of all ages; even the most important organisations of the 1970s, such as the 'Music Makers' and others, found it difficult to survive.

Many considered it more expedient to merge with either the 'Valley Boys' or the 'Saxons' than to compete with them. It was no longer feasible for any new group, however full of potential, to compete on the level of the major groups; and the battle for top place, fought between the Valley Boys and the Saxons, lost much of its excitement.

The eighties thus saw a decline in the participation of individuals and scrap groups in Junkanoo, and the broadening influence of the super-groups over the development of the festival. These groups continued, with the exception of the Music Makers, to grow in size and power, and, at their instigation, the craft of Junkanoo was transformed into a breathtaking art. The influence of these groups became so strong, however, that by the end of the decade it was virtually impossible for any other organisation to have any creative impact on the festival. This fact, compounded by the rise of crime, the advent of live television coverage and the overcrowded nature of Bay Street, caused a decline in Junkanoo's public appeal.

Conclusion

Junkanoo Present and Future
The Spirit of Junkanoo Lives

Today, Junkanoo is in a state of flux. The regulation of the last three decades has created a parade which is beautiful to look at; the near-elimination of scrap has contributed much to this beauty, for in the groups, even the most humble member is gorgeously costumed. In addition, the increasing involvement of professionals in the festival — artists, architects, engineers, musicians — has resulted in the ever-more precise turn-out of paraders. The sound produced by the rushers these days can by no means be considered 'noise'; the largest groups compete with full brass sections, which play songs related to their themes. Even the junkanoo rhythm has been adjusted to suit the parade's new, polished appearance. The eighties saw the development of a variety of fast beats. which, when combined with the tunes played on the horns, provide an exciting rhythmic accompaniment. Even more remarkable is the orderliness of the junkanoos themselves, a strong contast to the rowdiness of the forties. These days, as the saying goes, "it's safer to be on the street"; if a fight breaks out at Junkanoo, it is more likely to take place in the crowd than among the paraders.

The beginning of the 1990s has brought a challenge to the joint dominance of the Saxons and the Valley Boys. Becoming more and more visible is a new type of competitor — the community group. Smaller than the super-groups but modelled on their principles of organisation, community groups are made up of members of a certain neighbourhood, and are active throughout the year. In this, they continue the custom of rushing for a district. They are also socially responsible; they often use the preparation for Junkanoo as a time during which they instill discipline and a love for tradition in youngsters from their communities. All of them, however, attempt to set a standard of excellence in Junkanoo on a scale which is more generally accessible than that of the major competitors.

Against these positive developments are weighed those things which have made Junkanoo less popular in recent years. The lack of group competition is one; these days, all pretence of secrecy has been dropped by the major groups, who have taken to advertising their themes to draw crowds. In addition, unruly spectators, a congested route, and crowded sidewalks all make the parade difficult to see and, frequently, dangerous to attend. It is in these areas that the National Junkanoo Committee has been concentrating its most recent efforts.

Perhaps the most notorious of the Committee's attempts to improve parade conditions was its decision to remove Junkanoo from Bay Street. In September 1989, it was announced that, as Junkanoo seemed to have outgrown the city, it would be transferred to the Queen Elizabeth Sports Centre, where it might develop more fully; the first parade there would take place on Boxing Day. The pronouncement

Exhausted Dancer (Mr and Mrs W. Wong, Nassau)

came as a surprise to many, and the local papers were flooded with letters debating the issue. Meanwhile, a large number of junkanoos organised a protest, and gathered on Bay Street, chanting to the beat of their drums: "Bay Street forever! Sports Centre never!" The Junkanoo Committee, taken aback by the ferocity of the opposition, reversed the decision, and the parade was allowed to remain on Bay Street. Instead, the Committee proposed that the 1990–91 parade route be lengthened to accommodate the number of participants.

Perhaps the most ironic about the decision was its parallels with the 1942 riots. The Queen Elizabeth Sports Centre is built on the ruins of the old Oakes Airfield, one of the two bases chosen for the 1942 Project; and although the junkanoos' protest was peaceful, it took place in Rawson Square, the site of the riots' beginning. Finally, the Junkanoo Committee's surprise at the proposal's reception mirrors the colonial government's astonishment at the labourers' uprising — evidence, perhaps, that, even in an era of self-government, leaders are still capable of underestimating the public will.

And, as my father pointed out in his thesis, that will is strong where Junkanoo is concerned:

> Junkanoo music lies at the very core of the Bahamian mentality and as such is central to his being. Whenever Bahamians feel the need to celebrate an event of deep significance or national import they do so with Junkanoo music. For example, when Sidney Poitier, the Bahamian actor, was awarded an Oscar for his performance in "Lilies of the Field", he was greeted at Nassau International Airport by numerous bands playing Junkanoo music; when in 1967, it was learnt that the predominantly white ruling minority Party had been overthrown by the present Government, the sounds of Junkanoo music echoed throughout the city; and when in 1973, The Bahamas gained its Independence and became a sovereign nation, the event was marked by performances of Junkanoo music.

Over a decade has passed since my father wrote those words, and many things have changed. Nevertheless, Junkanoo remains essential to the cultural identity of many Bahamians. Since Independence, indeed, we have become more conscious of its existence. The organisation of the festival has made it acceptable to all members of society; women, children and white Bahamians have all become regular participants. At the same time, as we have seen, the political power of the celebration has grown more and more evident, and in recent years, Bahamians have begun taking note of the festival's commercial power. Junkanoo remains a popular subject for paintings and photographs, and has inspired the development of a new fine art form: in the past few years Junkanoo 'paintings' and sculptures — designs made in the same way

as junkanoo costumes, but on the more intimate scale of conventional art — have been introduced and have proved popular. The 1980s also saw Junkanoo become the subject of considerable research, by Americans in search of their festival's roots as well as by Bahamians. At home, there is a marked interest in its development, and the celebration is increasingly studied in schools. In 1988, therefore, partly to encourage this trend, and partly to foster new approaches to the festival, the first Junior Junkanoo Parade, an annual inter-school competition, took place. Despite drawbacks, the festival is far from dying.

What then of the future?

In The Bahamas, Junkanoo has transcended slavery and emancipation, poverty and wealth, racial discrimination and social equality; it is unlikely, then, that it will not outlast the present. That is not to say that it will remain the same. The purpose of this book has been to show, in part, how closely the festival is tied to the social history of the nation; as the fortunes of the Bahamian people change, so does Junkanoo. The present glory of the parades, indeed, may be said to reflect the modern preoccupation with material goods — hence the brilliance of the costumes, the catchiness of the music, the massive proportions of the groups and the general showiness of the event. It is by no means certain, however, that Junkanoo will remain thus, despite the large sums of money now spent on it by the major groups or the prognostications of the Junkanoo Committee.

In all, though, certain constants remain. First, Bahamian Junkanoo is an urban festival. It is a tradition which was celebrated, from the days of slavery, in Nassau alone. It is a tradition, moreover, which could have developed only in the tightly-knit communities of the city slaves. The individualistic John Canoe figures which populated other New World territories, like the 'Old Neptune' characters which appeared in the southern Bahamas, did not endure long in Nassau; there, Junkanoo was celebrated by the community. Bahamian Junkanoo is, above all, a festival of the city.

Junkanoo is also a symbol of protest. From its earliest manifestation to the present day, it has been a celebration which has taken place in spite of the status quo. It has also, since its earliest recognition in Nassau, taken place in the 'market' — in the heart, that is, of the rulers' power. It is not far-fetched to suggest that, for the junkanoos of the pre-Independence years, the annual occupation of Bay Street represented their protest against their disenfranchisement, and that protest is still implicit in the modern parade. The continued survival of scrap, however slim, recalls Junkanoo's unorthodox origin; and even today, many of the men who 'rush' still have no power in the city in ordinary life. To remove Junkanoo from the market, then, is to deny its symbolism for all Bahamians.

Finally, Junkanoo is a custom of the people. It is not subject to the decrees of government, nor is it the property, even, of the leaders of the Junkanoo groups. On the contrary, it rests in the hearts of ordinary Nassauvians, and it is they who create it.

And the spirit of Junkanoo lives. It is not a spirit which resides in the Conference Room at the Ministry of Youth where the National Junkanoo Committee meets, or even among the Junkanoo leaders; it is not a spirit which bows to the will of anyone who sees it as a duty to 'develop' Junkanoo. The spirit of Junkanoo is one of independence and pride. It is the memory of a people, and as such cannot be regulated; it is found in the fantasies which occupy Bay Street twice a year, and has its heart in the beat of the goombay drum. It is, as my father once wrote, "deeply rooted in the cultural heritage of the Bahamian people and as such represents their past, their present and their aspirations for the future."

Egyptian Costume (Mr K. McClary, Dublin)

Index